# Plough Quarterly

BREAKING GROUND FOR A RENEWED WO

Autumn 2016, Number 10

## Feature: What Makes Humans Sacred?

## Reviews and Essays

**Artists:** Pawel Kuczynski, Xenia Hausner, William H. Johnson, Käthe Kollwitz, Deidre Scherer, Jason Landsel

# Plough Quarterly

WWW.PLOUGH.COM

## Meet the community behind Plough.

*Plough Quarterly* is published by the Bruderhof, an international community of people seeking to follow Jesus together. Members of the Bruderhof are committed to a way of radical discipleship in the spirit of the Sermon on the Mount. Inspired by the first church in Jerusalem (Acts 2 and 4), members renounce private property and share everything in common in a life of service to God, one another, and neighbors near and far.

The community includes families and single people from a wide range of backgrounds, with around 2,700 people in all. There are twenty-three Bruderhof settlements in both rural and urban locations in the United States, England, Germany, Australia, and Paraguay.

To learn more, arrange a visit, or check out blogs or videos with perspectives from Bruderhof members, see the community's website at *bruderhof.com.*

*Plough Quarterly* features original stories, ideas, and culture to inspire everyday faith and action. Starting from the conviction that the teachings and example of Jesus can transform and renew our world, we aim to apply them to all aspects of life, seeking common ground with all people of goodwill regardless of creed. The goal of *Plough Quarterly* is to build a living network of readers, contributors, and practitioners so that, in the words of Hebrews, we may "spur one another on toward love and good deeds."

*Plough Quarterly* includes contributions that we believe are worthy of our readers' consideration, whether or not we fully agree with them. Views expressed by contributors are their own and do not necessarily reflect the editorial position of Plough or of the Bruderhof communities.

Editors: Peter Mommsen, Sam Hine, Maureen Swinger. Art director: Emily Alexander. Online editor: Erna Albertz.
Contributing editors: Charles E. Moore, Chungyon Won, Yacoub Yousif, Marianne Wright.
Founding Editor: Eberhard Arnold (1883–1935).

*Plough Quarterly No. 10: What Makes Humans Sacred?*
Published by Plough Publishing House, ISBN 978-0-87486-819-7
Copyright © 2016 by Plough Publishing House. All rights reserved.

Scripture quotations (unless otherwise noted) are from the New Revised Standard Version Bible, copyright © 1989 the Division of Christian Education of the National Council of the Churches of Christ in the United States of America. Used by permission. All rights reserved.

Inside front cover: Pawel Kuczynski, *Islands*, 2015. © Pawel Kuczynski. Used by permission of the artist. *pawelkuczynski.com*

| Editorial Office | Subscriber Services | United Kingdom | Australia |
|---|---|---|---|
| PO Box 398 | PO Box 345 | Brightling Road | 4188 Gwydir Highway |
| Walden, NY 12586 | Congers, NY 10920-0345 | Robertsbridge | Elsmore, NSW |
| T: 845.572.3455 | T: 800.521.8011 | TN32 5DR | 2360 Australia |
| *info@plough.com* | *subscriptions@plough.com* | T: +44(0)1580.883.344 | T: +61(0)2.6723.2213 |

*Plough Quarterly* (ISSN 2372-2584) is published quarterly by Plough Publishing House, PO Box 398, Walden, NY 12586.
Individual subscription $32 per year in the United States; Canada add $8, other countries add $16.
Periodicals postage paid at Walden, NY 12586 and at additional mailing offices.
POSTMASTER: Send address changes to *Plough Quarterly*, PO Box 345, Congers, NY 10920-0345.

# Humans Are . . . Sacred?

## Dear Reader,

The gospel teaches that every human is sacred. It's a far from obvious claim. Consider what it means: orange-haired casino owners, former First Ladies, judo-loving foreigners called Vladimir, and aging *comandantes* – each of them sacred.

Muslim refugee children are sacred. So are the Islamist terrorists who (some fear) they may become. Police officers are sacred, as are young African Americans with names like Trayvon Martin, Eric Garner, and Freddie Gray. Unborn babies are sacred, always. And so too, with all their grave guilt, are abortionists. Progressive hipsters, prosperity-gospel televangelists, members of Congress, gender-transitioning former decathletes, Confederate-flag-waving white nationalists? Sacred.

This absurd claim is the joyful surprise at the heart of the gospel. Each person, just or unjust, is created in the image and likeness of God. Each is someone for whom Jesus died. As Christians our faith only makes sense if the proposition that humans are sacred is true.

And if it is true, we have much work to do. Despite the proliferation of human rights talk, our society is busy dismantling respect for human sacredness. Our political debates reflect this. Enthusiasm for torture and for carpet-bombing civilians on the right is mirrored by #ShoutYourAbortion and celebrations of euthanasia on the left. In June 2016, the US Supreme Court's *Whole Woman's Health vs. Hellerstedt* decision dashed hopes that this

country's abortion license might at least be narrowed. Meanwhile no major US politician seems interested in the three million children living in the extreme poverty documented in the book *$2.00 a Day.*

Recent months have made clear that any influence American Christians may once have wielded in public affairs has mostly evaporated. The causes for Christianity's marginalization can be debated – sexual revolution fallout? neoliberalism and social fragmentation? backlash against Christians' still-unrepented support for Bush-era wars? – but its reality is undeniable.

It's encouraging, then, to turn for guidance to another time when Christianity was politically sidelined: the church of the first three centuries, when the faith was still illegal. As Ronald J. Sider reminds us (page 34), these early believers lived out their belief in the sacredness of humans in a strikingly countercultural way: they refused to kill, ever. They insisted: Christians do not go to war, they do not participate in the death penalty, they do not practice abortion or infanticide, they do not watch violent entertainment.

Yet the early church's pro-life witness went beyond refusing to kill. As even their enemies admitted, Christians were known for their self-sacrificial willingness to care for the poor, the imprisoned, the sick, and the abandoned. Some are said to have sold themselves into slavery to help others.

> **"Killing a human being is always wrong because it is God's will for man to be a sacred creature."**
>
> Lactantius, AD 311

Artwork: Josh Sarantitis, *Reach High and You Will Go Far,* mural at 20th and Arch Street, Philadelphia, 2000

What if Christians' pro-life witness was just as robust today? What if we responded to the church's marginalization by recapturing our recklessness for life? Imagine the stir if all Christians refused to kill for any reason – why not leave "just war" to secular folks? – and if the church became known for its self-sacrificing love. There are a host of forerunners to show us the way, from Francis of Assisi to Florence Nightingale to Mother Teresa.

We need consistency – what Joseph Cardinal Bernardin, in a famous 1983 lecture, called "a consistent ethic of life." Bernardin, like Pope Francis today, appealed to opponents of abortion to prove their belief in the sacredness of life by also standing up for "the old and the young, the hungry and the homeless, the undocumented immigrant, and the unemployed worker."

> "Christianity provides a unified answer for the whole of life."
>
> Francis Schaeffer

Critics were quick to charge that Bernardin's definition of consistency was so broad that it risked downplaying the unique horrors of abortion. It might, they feared, lead to pro-abortion politicians coopting the pro-life label while cherry-picking just those issues they found convenient to support (for example, death penalty abolition, nuclear disarmament, or anti-poverty programs). This fear would prove well-grounded.

Yet the real problem isn't too much consistency in defending life, but too little. After all, Bernardin's words seem cautious and mild compared to the bracing message of Tertullian, Cyprian, the *Didache,* or the Sermon on the Mount. The early Christians were little interested in nudging public policy this way or that; they were building something both simpler and grander. As Francis Schaeffer remarked in regard to abortion, "We should have in mind not only this important issue as though it stood alone. . . . Christianity provides a unified answer for the whole of life."

What does this unified answer look like? As Erna Albertz's story illustrates (page 16), it means seeking to live out all of Jesus' teachings, especially those that have been dismissed as impossible and unrealistic. Eberhard Arnold puts it well:

> Even the killing of unborn life, a Massacre of the Innocents that today is multiplied a thousandfold, remains unassailable apart from faith in the kingdom of God. The supposedly high culture of our day will continue to carry out this massacre as long as social disorder and injustice still exist. The murder of unborn children cannot be stopped as long as public and private life are allowed to remain as they are.
>
> We can demand neither purity in marriage nor the end of infanticide unless we are willing to oppose private property and the lie of unjust social stratification with a realistic alternative: that is, we must prove that a different way of life is possible. Christian morality cannot be demanded outside the context of a way of life whose name is "the kingdom of God" and "the church of Jesus Christ." (*Innenland,* 1936)

I hope the articles in this issue will rekindle your zeal and joy in building up such a way of life. The writers don't all agree on the best ways and means, but each challenges us to consider: isn't the unadulterated gospel of life an answer whose time has come?

Warm greetings,

*Peter*

Peter Mommsen
*Editor*

*On Tom Sine's "Live Like You Give a Damn," Summer 2016 digital edition:* Churches were filled by silent promises: join our church and we promise never to make you uncomfortable, never to ask you to really change, never to bring you close to the people and issues you fear, never to ask you to get comfortable with dying – certainly not dying daily to self. . . . We need to be truthful about how we filled all those edifices, and accept that the false advertising has come home to roost.

*Rev. Margaret G. Crandall, Durham, NC*

Forget "sacred" or "secular" – if it is an action for justice, it is of God (perhaps unless it involves violence, but I am not sure about that – lots of violence in the Old Testament). Christians should be involved in the struggle for justice alongside whomever will work with them. Maybe like Gideon's army, God only needs a few Christians in the developed world and the church is growing where it is needed.

*Michael Smathers, Crossville, TN*

*On Norann Voll's "Why I Love to Wear a Head Covering," Summer 2016:* The clothes you choose to wear do not necessarily make you closer to Christ. The Bible has to be read with discernment and the customs do not all apply today. It was common for women in the Middle East at that time to cover their hair. It was also OK to keep slaves! What woman today would think it inappropriate to wear pearls, apply makeup, or wear attractive clothes?

*Annette Young, London, UK*

I am a liberal Christian and actively support all women trying to throw off cultural patriarchy to embrace their freedom in Christ. However, this was a wonderfully written article. It was irenic and informative. The author's use of logic and scripture never seemed like a back-door way to shame others who disagree. This is the way brothers and sisters should talk about their differences.

*David Taylor*

---

*We welcome letters to the editor. Letters and web comments may be edited for length and clarity, and may be published in any medium. Letters should be sent with the writer's name and address to letters@plough.com.*

Marianne Stokes, *Candlemas Day*

## The Benedict Option and Hauerwas

*On his* American Conservative *blog, Rod Dreher responded to Stanley Hauerwas's remarks in* Plough's *Summer 2016 issue:*

I was pleased to see that you addressed my Benedict Option idea. My suspicion is that there is less distance between your views and mine than you may think. I want to clarify that in my own thinking about the Benedict Option, I am not advocating an Amish-style withdrawal from the world (though I respect those who feel called to it, and wish them well). That will not be the path for most of us, nor, in my view, should it be. I am calling for more of a conscious "exile in place" for the church – that is, for the kind of Christians I call small-O orthodox Christians. Some people may need to physically move for this kind of community, but in most cases (I think) it will be a matter of deepening one's commitments to one's own tradition and the church community in which it is embodied, and in thickening the bonds among the community's members. This requires a clear understanding that our first loyalty is to the church, not to American empire. . . .

People are struggling to know what to do. I have kids of my own, and I am not content to sit back and accept what the empire has planned for them. I want to encourage and cultivate faithful Christian resistance. ➤

*Read the full post: theamericanconservative.com/dreher/hauerwas-vs-the-benedict-option*

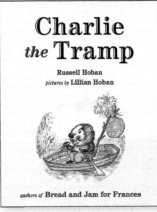

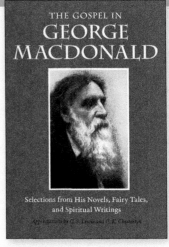

## Who wouldn't want to be a tramp?

Charlie the Beaver wants to be a tramp when he grows up: "Tramps don't have to learn how to chop down trees and how to roll logs and how to build dams. Tramps just tramp around and have a good time." Charlie sets off with his bundle, but when he hears water trickling, he can't get to sleep. Will he be able to resist the urge to make it stop? As Grandfather Beaver says, "You never know when a tramp will turn out to be a beaver."

Like many parents looking for quality children's literature, we find ourselves returning to the stand-out books of our own childhood. So we were thrilled to acquire this old favorite by the authors of *Bread and Jam for Frances* and make it available in a 50th anniversary hardcover edition.

## Our hero is back!

The young prince with Down syndrome who starred in Plough's award-winning 2015 book *The Prince Who Was Just Himself* is ready for school. In his kingdom, children go to school on sailing ships. There is a ship for girls and one for boys. There is a ship for children with an eye patch, a ship for children with one leg, and a ship for children who don't learn as fast. No one knows why there are so many different ships, but it has always been that way.

Then a terrible storm drives the ships into the hands of pirates. The boys and girls realize that they will only escape if everyone does what he or she does best. This delightfully illustrated fairy tale instills appreciation for children with developmental challenges.

## Finding the Gospel in Fairy Tales

Don't miss the latest in Plough's "The Gospel in Great Writers" series, an anthology that distills the Christian vision of the great Scottish storyteller George MacDonald (see page 76).

Image from Wikimedia Commons (public domain)

Paula Modersohn-Becker, *Girl with Red Dress and Sunflower*

## Consistent Life Network

Eileen Egan, a founder of Pax Christi USA and a close friend of Dorothy Day, is credited with first describing the Christian's defense of every life as a "seamless garment," a reference to the clothing taken from Jesus at the crucifixion. She wrote, "In common with the early followers of Jesus, we view the protection of all life, from its conception to its end, as a seamless garment."

In 1987 the Seamless Garment Network was established to unite organizations and individuals committed to advocating for a "consistent life ethic." Although the term has occasionally proved convenient cover for politicians more committed to some life issues than others, the organization is determined to remain non-partisan. In 2002 it changed its name to Consistent Life Network to reflect a move toward a broader interfaith membership.

"We are committed to the protection of life, which is threatened in today's world by war, abortion, poverty, racism, the death penalty, and euthanasia. . . . We challenge those working on all or some of these issues to maintain a cooperative spirit of peace, reconciliation, and respect in protecting the unprotected. . . . We serve the anti-violence community by connecting issues, building bridges, and strengthening the case against each kind of socially-approved killing by consistently opposing them all."
*consistentlifenetwork.org*

## You Carried Me

Melissa Ohden is fourteen when she learns that she is the survivor of a botched abortion. In this intimate memoir, which Plough will be releasing in January, she details her search for her biological parents and her own journey from anger and shame to faith and forgiveness.

After a decade-long search Ohden finally locates her birth father and writes to extend forgiveness, only to learn that he has died without answering her burning questions. Years later, she finally hears from the woman who carried her and gave her life – and was never told that the child she was forced to abort had survived.

Yet even the most startling family secrets are eclipsed by the triumphant moment when Ohden becomes a mother herself in the very hospital where she was aborted. And she reveals how – through the miscarriage of her only son and the birth of a second daughter with complex health issues, and through hearing her own birth mother's story – she has gained a deep empathy for every woman impacted by abortion.

This intensely personal story of love and redemption cuts through the debates surrounding a divisive issue to touch our common humanity. The sensitivity with which Ohden personalizes issues such as adoption and women's rights will appeal to readers regardless of their views. *youcarriedmebook.com*

## Poet in This Issue: Joseph Michael Fino

A member of the Franciscan Friars of the Renewal, Brother Joseph Michael Fino lives in the South Bronx in New York City. His poem, "An Apology for Vivian" appears on page 67. ⤳

The nonviolent activist and priest Daniel Berrigan at Cornell University, 1970. In April 2016, just weeks after the Vatican convened a conference on nonviolence, Berrigan died at age ninety-four (see overleaf).

# Death Knell for Just War

## The Vatican's Historic Turn toward Nonviolence

**JOHN DEAR**

For its first three centuries, Christianity required the practice of active nonviolence as taught by Jesus. Early Christians refused to serve in Rome's armies or kill in its wars. All that changed in the year 313, when Emperor Constantine legalized

camps, prayed for successful bombing raids, and built and used nuclear weapons. Jesus' teachings of nonviolence have rarely been discussed, much less implemented. Even as recent popes have proclaimed a "Gospel of Life," they've made exceptions, leaving loopholes for justified killing.

That may be about to change. In April, eighty prominent Catholic peacemakers from twenty-five nations were invited to the Vatican for a conference to discuss formally abandoning the just war theory. The event was hosted by the Pontifical Council for Justice and Peace. Cardinal Peter Turkson, the leader behind Pope Francis's recent encyclical on the environment, opened the conference by reading a long letter of welcome from Pope Francis. Cardinal Turkson participated in the conference and approved the closing

Christianity, and established it as the official religion of the empire. In effect, he threw out the commandment to love one's enemies and turned to the pagan Cicero to justify Christian violence, sowing the seeds for the so-called just war theory.

During the seventeen centuries since, Christians have waged war, led crusades, burned women at the stake, persecuted Jews and Muslims, kept slaves, run concentration statement, which was then presented to the pope.

For three days, we deliberated about questions of violence, war, and nonviolence. Many attendees shared personal experiences practicing nonviolence, often in warzones. I was asked to speak about Jesus and nonviolence. That's easy, I said: Jesus did not teach us how to kill or wage war or make money; he taught us how to be nonviolent. In the Sermon on the Mount he

---

*John Dear, a Catholic priest, is the author of thirty books on peace and nonviolence, including* Walking the Way, Living Peace, *and his latest,* The Beatitudes of Peace. johndear.org

says: "Blessed are the peacemakers, they are the sons and daughters of God. . . . You have heard it said, thou shall not kill; I say to you, do not even get angry. . . . You have heard it said, an eye for an eye; but I say to you, offer no violent resistance to one who does evil. . . . Love your enemies." Nowhere does he say: " . . . but if your enemies are really bad, and you meet these seven conditions, kill them." There is no just war theory, there are no exceptions.

During the closing hours we debated, approved, and released a statement calling on Pope Francis to write an encyclical that would formally reject the just war theory once and for all and return the Church to the nonviolence of Jesus. The statement offers four points: that Jesus was nonviolent; that there is no just war; that nonviolence works; and that the time has come for the Church to apply and teach nonviolence at every level around the world. To quote some highlights:

"We live in a time of tremendous suffering, widespread trauma and fear linked to militarization, economic injustice, climate change, and a myriad of other specific forms of violence. In this context of normalized and systemic violence, those of us who stand in the Christian tradition are called to recognize the centrality of active nonviolence to the vision and message of Jesus; to the life and practice of the Catholic Church; and to our long-term vocation of healing and reconciling both people and the planet. . . .

REMEMBERING

# Daniel Berrigan

**JOHN DEAR**

Apart from the Vatican conference on peacemaking, April 2016 also marked the passing of one of the great peacemakers of our age. Daniel Berrigan, the renowned antiwar activist and Jesuit priest who inspired religious opposition to war and nuclear weapons, died April 30, just a week shy of his ninety-fifth birthday.

Berrigan was my greatest friend and teacher for over thirty-five years. We traveled the nation and the world together, went to jail together; I edited five books of his writings. In one of our first conversations he said to me, "The whole point is to make one's life make sense in light of the gospel, to get your life to fit into the story of the gospel."

During his lifetime Berrigan published over fifty books of poetry, essays, and scripture commentaries, but he will be remembered best for the day he lit the match that ignited widespread national protest against the Vietnam War. On May 17, 1968, along with his brother Philip and seven others, Berrigan burned draft files in Catonsville, Maryland, with homemade napalm to protest the war. "Our apologies, good friends," he wrote, "for the fracture of good order, the burning of paper instead of children, the angering of the orderlies in the

Photograph courtesy of Jim Forest

"The time has come for our church to be a living witness and to invest far greater human and financial resources in promoting a spirituality and practice of active nonviolence and in forming and training our Catholic communities in effective nonviolent practices. In all of this, Jesus is our inspiration and model.

"In his own times, rife with structural violence, Jesus proclaimed a new, nonviolent order rooted in the unconditional love of God. . . . Neither passive nor weak, Jesus' nonviolence was the power of love in action. In vision and deed, he is the revelation and embodiment of the nonviolent God, a truth especially illuminated in the cross and resurrection. He calls us to develop the virtue of nonviolent peacemaking.

"Clearly, the Word of God, the witness of Jesus, should never be used to justify violence, injustice, or war. We confess that the people of God have betrayed this central message of the gospel many times, by participating in wars, persecution, oppression, exploitation, and discrimination.

"We believe that there is no just war. Too often the just war theory has been used to endorse rather than prevent or limit war. Suggesting that a just war is possible also undermines the moral imperative to develop tools and capacities for nonviolent transformation of conflict. We need a new framework that is consistent with gospel nonviolence. . . ."

Among other points, the statement specifically challenges the church to develop its social

front parlor of the charnel house. We could not, so help us God, do otherwise."

The action attracted massive press coverage and led to hundreds of similar demonstrations. In his autobiography *To Dwell in Peace,* Berrigan reflected on the effect of the Catonsville protest:

The act was pitiful, a tiny flare amid the consuming fires of war. But Catonsville was like a firebreak, a small fire lit, to contain and conquer a greater. The time, the place, were weirdly right. They spoke for passion, symbol, reprisal. Catonsville seemed to light up the dark places of the heart, where courage and risk and hope were awaiting a signal, a dawn. For the remainder of our lives, the fires would burn and burn, in hearts and minds, in draft boards, in prisons and courts. A new fire, new as a Pentecost, flared up in eyes deadened and hopeless, the noble powers of soul given over to the "powers of the upper air." "Nothing can be done!" How often we had

heard that gasp: the last of the human, of soul, of freedom. Indeed, something could be done, and was. And would be.

In his 1969 bestseller, *No Bars to Manhood,* Berrigan wrote:

We have assumed the name of peacemakers, but we have been, by and large, unwilling to pay any significant price. And because we want the peace with half a heart and half a life and will, the war, of course, continues, because the waging of war, by its nature, is total – but the waging of peace, by our own cowardice, is partial. . . . There is no peace because there are no peacemakers. There are no makers of peace because the making of peace is at least as costly as the making of war – at least as exigent, at least as disruptive, at least as liable to bring disgrace and prison and death in its wake.

On September 9, 1980, Berrigan opened a new chapter in the history of nonviolent resistance. Drawing inspiration from the biblical prophet

teaching on nonviolence; to promote nonviolent practices such as restorative justice, trauma healing, and unarmed civilian protection; to no longer use or teach just war theory; to continue advocating for the abolition of war and nuclear weapons; and to support and defend nonviolent activists whose work for peace and justice puts their lives at risk. I encourage you to read the full statement at *nonviolencejustpeace.net.*

If it heeds this call, the Catholic Church could change course from the last seventeen

> ## "The death of a single human is too heavy a price to pay for the vindication of any principle, however sacred."
>
> Daniel Berrigan

hundred years, opening up a whole new history for Christianity and returning us to the spirit of the early church, where no Christian was allowed to participate in war, prepare for war, or kill another human being. If Pope Francis writes such an encyclical, it could have an impact far beyond the world's one billion Catholics. He could help us all better understand how war has become obsolete, how nonviolence offers far better prospects for conflict resolution, and why the time has come to abolish war and nuclear weapons. ⮞

Isaiah – "They shall beat their swords into plowshares and their spears into pruning hooks" – he and Philip and six friends walked into a General Electric plant in King of Prussia, Pennsylvania, and hammered on unarmed nuclear weapon nosecones. They were arrested, tried, convicted, and faced up to ten years in prison for destruction of government property.

Berrigan exemplifies a Christianity that works for peace, speaks for peace, and welcomes Christ's gift of peace. His life work, he would say, was modest. But the cumulative effect of his writings and actions show us what the church might look like, what a Christian looks like in such times, indeed, what a human response looks like in an inhuman world. From the days of the "war on communism" to the even darker days of the "war on terror," from the Cold War doctrine of "mutually assured destruction" to "shock and awe" in Iraq, Berrigan steadfastly said no to war, empire, and nuclear weapons. At the same time, through

his poetry, books, retreats, and talks – indeed by his very life – he offered an affirming yes to the God of life and peace. He understood that you can't have one without the other.

I consider Daniel Berrigan not just a legendary peace activist but one of the greatest saints and prophets of modern times. He waged peace with his whole heart, will, and life, and paid the cost. Time and time again he was denounced and exiled, arrested and imprisoned, and yet he continued to stand at the center of the culture of war with the good news of Christ the peacemaker. In a world brimming with death he was a witness to resurrection. We don't need to canonize him, but we need to take seriously his life, his commitment to the Word, his faith in the God of peace, and his steadfast resistance to evil. His witness gives us hope that we too can be instruments of God's peace and join with the saints and martyrs of history to give birth to a new world without war, injustice, or nuclear weapons. ⮞

# My Return to Iraq

## Twenty-six years after fleeing Saddam Hussein, a former asylum seeker goes back to visit Christians on the run from ISIS.

### YACOUB YOUSIF

I was raised in a nominally Christian home in Baghdad, but it was as a foot soldier in Saddam Hussein's army during the Iran–Iraq War that I became convinced that as a follower of Jesus I could no longer kill or serve in the military. In 1990, with another war looming, I knew I would be called up again and that I faced execution if I refused to serve. I chose instead to flee Iraq with my wife, Layla, and our baby daughter. We received asylum in Sweden, and now are members of a Bruderhof community in England.

Naturally, the human tragedy sweeping the Middle East these days hits especially close to home. The crimes committed by ISIS and other factions that drive people, both Christians and Muslims, from their homes in Syria and Iraq cry to heaven. These are our people, and our hearts long to comfort them.

So we jumped at the chance when our church agreed to send us to Iraq for two months earlier this year to report on the situation of refugees and displaced people, and to encourage Christians suffering for their faith. When we landed in Erbil and stepped onto the soil of our homeland for the first time after so many years, we were overwhelmed, our tears of joy mixed with sorrow over all that has happened to our country.

We could not help noticing how decades of war have halted progress and dragged the country backward. The country's

The author and his wife, Layla, with an Iraqi Christian *(center)* who was injured while escaping ISIS fighters

---

*Yacoub Yousif is Plough's Arabic editor. He tells his own story in a memoir,* I Put My Sword Away: An Iraqi Soldier's Journey from Battlefield to Brotherhood *(Bruderhof, 2016).*

The Al-Amal Hope Center, an unfinished building in Erbil, houses Iraqis who fled Mosul after ISIS militants took control of the area.

infrastructure has been going downhill for twenty-five years. Kurdistan, in northern Iraq, had just begun to emerge from this devastation; we saw many signs of recent development and urbanization. But that mostly ground to a halt with the emergence of ISIS. Though this region borders ISIS strongholds, thousands of displaced people have sought refuge in its relatively safety, and even Christians from Baghdad have found it a temporary haven. This influx, along with increasing military expenditures, has caused intense economic pressure. On top of that, almost everyone we spoke to complained of corruption and the looting of state funds.

We visited several camps for displaced people – Muslims, Christians, and Yazidis. Outside the camps, sheltering wherever they could find space, were Christians from Mosul, the Nineveh plain, and Baghdad. The citizens of Kurdistan, though of different religions, have opened schools, halls, churches, and uninhabited houses to accommodate the torrent of refugees. Still, many end up on the streets, sleeping on the ground in people's yards and public parks.

We heard horrific stories of evictions from people who had left behind property, possessions, businesses, churches, and the graves of loved ones. It is hard to forget the story of one elderly woman who told us she had tripped and fallen when ISIS attacked her village; her legs have been paralyzed ever since. One family had already migrated within Iraq three times, fleeing first from skirmishes between ISIS and the Peshmerga, the Kurdish army, in their hometown, Qaraqosh. They took refuge in Sharanish, a remote village near the Turkish border, only to come under fire from Turkish airstrikes targeting Kurdish militants.

An eighty-five-year-old widow told us how she returned to her home in Mosul after visiting relatives. She didn't know what had happened but saw that there were no Christians and that all the men were bearded. She went and asked an imam what had happened to all the Christians. He replied that they all had to become Muslims. She said, "But I don't want to become a Muslim." To which he said, "Then you will be killed." She is now being cared for by the church in a small village in Kurdistan.

We also met people who had been kidnapped for ransom. One Christian man from Baghdad was kidnapped by his own neighbor, a man he had thought was a friend. He told us about the insults, false accusations, and brutal treatment he endured. A full week after payment of the ransom, he was finally released. A Christian woman told us about the day she set out to fetch her son from school. Since it looked like rain, she had brought along her umbrella. On the way, a car pulled up beside her and three armed men got out. They trained their machine guns on her and ordered her into the car. When she refused, one of them caught her by her long hair, wrapped his beefy hand in it, and yanked so vigorously that it was pulled out at the roots. As they tried to push her into the car, she prayed silently to the Virgin Mary, pleading for help. Unexpectedly, the umbrella popped open, momentarily making a barrier between her and her assailants. She broke free and fled to the nearest doorway as the men opened fire, hitting the

ground at her feet. The resident, a Muslim, opened his iron door and then locked it behind her, saving her from certain kidnapping.

In the midst of all this tragedy some surprisingly cheerful individuals stood out. In obtaining the pearl of great price – faith in Jesus Christ – these new Christians had been given an overwhelming joy despite their circumstances. They said they were no longer worried about their situation because their future was now in the hands of the Lord. Several testified that Jesus had saved them from death at the hands of extremists. We marveled to see in their jubilant faces the work of the Lord in this war-torn land. Shouldn't our prayer be that those who have driven these people from their homes find faith and repentance, too?

Most of the people we spoke with want to emigrate because they do not see a stable future in Iraq. This was not surprising. But we found others opposed to emigration on nationalist grounds. They would say to us, for example, "This is our country, our land and the land of our ancestors. Our history is here." Or, "We will not leave our homeland. We have sacrificed our blood for it, the blood of many martyrs in many wars." Or, "Have we killed so many of the enemy, so many ISIS troops, only to flee?"

This attitude, expressed so passionately, made Layla and me remember why we left Iraq. Didn't Jesus tell us to love our enemies? Is it not our calling as Christians to represent the peaceable kingdom of God here on earth? Although every homeland is precious, Christ and his church are our dearest treasure. If governments ask us to do evil things against the commandments of Jesus, we must obey God rather than men. When this brings persecution, sometimes we will have to stand firm, and sometimes we may have to flee.

We did not feel we could advise anyone whether to go or stay. We would pray with them for the guidance of the Holy Spirit. But we did urge them to stand together in solidarity as a Christian community, putting the principles of the kingdom of God into practice as a group: lifelong commitment, full dedication, total sharing, love to all people, and service to one another, their neighbors, and their country. For this is God's will for his people, and this is the most important testimony they can bring to the world: unity, solidarity, a shared future, and a shared destiny. The church of Christ is a united group, not a bunch of independent individuals who are not bound to one another. In every decision, we should give priority to the church, which represents the kingdom of God on earth as its holy embassy. ➤

Christians who fled Mosul worship at Erbil's Mar Shmony Church (June 2016).

# Pursuing Happiness

## How my sister with Down syndrome can help Richard Dawkins boost the sum of human joy

**ERNA ALBERTZ**

TWO YEARS AGO, a woman posed a hypothetical scenario to Richard Dawkins, the evolutionary biologist and well-known atheist, tweeting: "I honestly don't know what I would do if I were pregnant with a kid with Down syndrome. Real ethical dilemma."

Dawkins tweeted back seconds later: "Abort it and try again. It would be immoral to bring it into the world if you have the choice."

In the firestorm of outrage that followed, even many of Dawkins's fellow utilitarians disavowed his hundred-character pronouncement. The next day, Dawkins half-apologized

---

*Erna Albertz is Plough's online editor and a member of the Bruderhof. She lives with her sister Iris at the Woodcrest community in Rifton, New York.*

Xenia Hausner, *Blind Date*, 2009

in a statement on his website, but still did not back down: "Parents who care for their children with Down syndrome usually form strong bonds of affection with them, as they would with any child. . . . I have sympathy for this emotional point, but it is an emotional one, not a logical one. . . .

"If your morality is based, as mine is, on a desire to increase the sum of happiness and reduce suffering, the decision to deliberately give birth to a Down baby, when you have the choice to abort it early in the pregnancy, might actually be immoral from the point of view of the child's own welfare."[1]

> **The artist Xenia Hausner,** born in 1951, is a painter whose pictures focus on the mysterious world of human relationships, with all their unknowns, fragmentariness, and risk. Hausner is a member of Women without Borders, an organization that seeks to promote communication between women in Europe and the Arab world. She lives and works in Vienna and Berlin.

As advocates for people with disabilities were quick to point out, Dawkins's assumptions about Down syndrome are not borne out by research. A 2011 study, for instance, found that 99 percent of individuals with Down syndrome were happy with their lives, and that 97 percent of their parents and 94 percent of their siblings reported feelings of pride.[2] Only 5 percent of siblings were willing to trade their brother or sister with Down syndrome for a sibling without it.

Yet citing quality-of-life studies does not get to the root of Dawkins's argument for aborting babies with disabilities: the fear of suffering.

I understand and share this fear. If Richard Dawkins were to read these words, I'd want him to know that I appreciate his basic motive: "a desire to increase the sum of happiness and reduce suffering." At a time marked by the endless march of grim headlines, don't we need more people passionately working toward this goal?

The difficulty, of course, is that neither suffering nor happiness is objectively measureable; both are, to use Dawkins's own words, a matter of emotion, not of logic. How are we to determine who suffers more: a child with disabilities who possesses an uncomplicated joy in life, or an intellectually gifted child who has difficulty forging relationships? Aleksandr Solzhenitsyn famously wrote that "the line dividing good and evil cuts through the heart of every human being." Similarly, the line dividing happiness and suffering runs through each human heart. That includes the hearts not only of people like Richard Dawkins but also of people like my sister Iris.

Iris entered the world in 1982, when I was three and a half. The obstetrician diagnosed her with Down syndrome and predicted that she would never walk, talk, or make any meaningful contribution to our family or society. Too tactful to state his opinion outright, he nonetheless made it clear: my parents should not delay in committing Iris to an institution where she could receive lifetime care, and we could avoid a pointless disruption of our family life.

My parents refused, and Iris came home to live with us. Despite the extra challenges she brought, our family soon formed (to use Dawkins's words) "strong bonds of mutual affection" with her. Born with two serious heart conditions, Iris underwent two open-heart surgeries before her second birthday. Before and between operations, she suffered from chronic pneumonia and spent most of her days in an oxygen tent. Endless processions of therapists helped her learn to swallow, cough, move, sit, and speak.

Later, although she was healthier, Iris's routines remained demanding. Helping her to dress, cut her food, brush her teeth, prepare for the day, do her therapies and her homework, keep track of her belongings, end the day happily, and stay peacefully in bed at night were (and are) tasks that require time and patience. Psychologists who have tested her say she has an extremely low IQ. Since it often isn't possible to reason with her – and she can be quite stubborn – creativity and humor are often our only way out.

> Free from intellectual hubris, Iris seems able to perceive spiritual realities the rest of us cannot.

Our family life changed in other, less visible ways too. We've never been able to undertake the adventures that "typical" families can, let alone spontaneous outings. Daily problem-solving with Iris's teachers and caregivers took time and research, often squeezing out a broader social life. For my father and mother, who were already in their fifties when Iris was in kindergarten, the challenges of midlife compounded the fatigue of caring for a child with special needs. It wasn't always pretty.

As children, we were unaware of these extra burdens, which weighed on our parents. And like most parents of a child with disabilities, their worries about the future were complicated by the question of who would care for Iris when they grew old and died. Although life expectancy for people with Down syndrome used to

Photograph courtesy of the author

be in the late twenties to early thirties, today, thanks to medical innovation, it has risen to fifty or sixty years – an advance that presents its own challenges. In the United States, individuals with disabilities receive few federal and state services after age twenty-one, even though this is often the time when their needs become more complex. We were extremely lucky not to have financial worries – more about that later – but families we knew struggled to cover the costs of medicine, therapies, adaptive equipment, and sometimes live-in caregivers.

I can't sugarcoat it: disability is tough. But does this mean that Iris's life is primarily one of suffering? Would the rest of us have been happier without her?

Decide for yourself. Iris has a spunky, bubbly personality. She is drawn to others like a bee to nectar, effortlessly overcoming interpersonal barriers. We call her our "family ambassador" because she is always the first to go out of her way to connect with new people. Once she has established a relationship, we need only to say "We are Iris's family" to become fast friends. She sympathizes deeply with anyone in need: when she hears a news story about a violent incident halfway around the world, it hits her as though the victims were family.

Iris's contagious guffaw can enliven an entire concert hall. (We've joked that she could earn a handsome income as a laugh starter.) Whether or not she understands an attempted joke, she'll let loose without a moment's hesitation. She remembers the characters played by childhood friends in grade-school theater productions, and continues to address them decades later by their stage names. Including in church. After celebrating the Lord's Supper, church members customarily greet one another with the words "peace and unity." At one such occasion, Iris spotted a beloved classmate and

The author and her sister

her gravelly voice rang out, "Princess Gloriana! Peace and unity!"

In her freedom from intellectual hubris, Iris seems able to perceive spiritual realities the rest of us cannot. Once a close friend of hers who had moved abroad – I'll call her Sandra – was especially on Iris's mind. For weeks, Iris asked me repeatedly how Sandra was doing. In exasperation one day I said, "Let's phone her and see!" Hearing Iris's voice on the line, Sandra was incredulous. "You know, I just heard today that my dad passed away. He's been very sick in hospital for a while now. Thank you so much for calling."

Another friend Iris took to mentioning incessantly was a woman I'll call Eleanor. We all got tired of hearing, over and over, how amazing Eleanor was. One day, to our shock, we received news that Eleanor had been diagnosed with late-stage cancer. I wondered if we'd been deaf to an urgent message Iris had insistently tried to convey: treasure Eleanor and pray for her.

When someone like Richard Dawkins looks in on families like mine, he sees only the challenges and assumes all is dark. I don't blame him for this blindness. Although I love my sister fiercely, she did not always seem a good and perfect gift to me. Growing up, I was sometimes frustrated by the demands her care made on us, and on a few occasions I found myself longing for a "normal" life. I regarded these infrequent bouts of self-pity as harmless and as having no bearing on my fundamental love for her. One day, however, I realized my attitude was not as innocent as I believed.

As a twenty-two-year-old, having left home four years earlier, I was living in Germany with my life before me. Like almost all young women of my generation, I embraced the notion that personal independence and a successful career were the route to happiness. Although I had grown up in a Christian home and still loved God, autonomy and success became part of my creed.

I decided to study midwifery, and as preparation volunteered at an obstetrics and gynecology hospital in the university town of Leipzig. On my first day on duty, I responded to the call bell and found myself in a private room with a woman in her mid-thirties. At the time, I was aware that abortions were legal at up to twenty-three weeks if a doctor diagnosed serious congenital malformations and signed a release for the procedure. I was also theoretically open to the idea that abortion might be justified in certain extreme circumstances – though obviously not for infants with Down syndrome, who (I thought) would never count as "severely disabled." How naïve I was.

> Is it feminist to tell a woman that she is tough enough to kill her own child, yet not tough enough to raise it?

When I entered the room, I did not know a late-term abortion was underway. The patient asked for help in going to the toilet. Though unfamiliar with the protocol to follow, I instinctively ran for a bedpan. Several minutes later, I caught a tiny bluish form – her son, unmistakably a human being, with arms, legs, ears, eyebrows, fingernails. He had died in utero following the injection of a toxic solution, and had then been expelled after nurses induced labor with a drip. The woman, seeing me speechless as I held the bedpan, explained: "The doctor told me it would have Down syndrome. I knew I couldn't handle that alone."

She must have sensed my distress. Trying to reassure me, she added: "Don't worry, I'm not a sissy. I'm tough and I can deal with this."

I called for a nurse. She clamped and cut the cord, her scissors separating mother from baby in a macabre mimicry of what would otherwise have been a moment of joy. Then she instructed me to place the bedpan in the sluice room where waste was collected. Hesitantly, I asked what would become of it. "Oh, they'll take it to the laboratory and use the tissue for research," she replied as she casually covered his remains with a paper towel.

In this hospital, the Premature Intensive Care Unit was located one floor below gynecology. There, no efforts were spared in the often frantic attempt to save twenty-four-week-old babies' lives. How, I wondered, did a life that was legally defined as a disposable fetus at twenty-three weeks become a human being at twenty-four?

With hours still left on my shift, I tried to pull myself together and act

Xenia Hausner, *Crime Map*, 2010

professionally – which apparently worked, since the staff later complimented me on how well I had handled it. But something in me was shattered. If my goals demanded tough choices, I had thought, then so be it. Until now, I had not realized just what the price of choice might be, and who might be forced to pay it.

As the cold reality of what I had witnessed sank in, I was filled with angry questions. If she was "alone," where was the man who had abandoned her? Had she been pressured by relatives, friends, or doctors? I was angry for the child who had not been able to defend himself, and angry that it was now too late.

If only I had met his mother just days earlier, I told myself, I could have told her about Iris.

But what would I have said? I began to rethink my worldview from the ground up. Is encouraging a woman to believe she is tough

enough to kill her own child, yet not tough enough to raise it, really standing up for her best interests? Isn't this actually just another way of putting a woman's needs last, so that when all is said and done, she is left to bear responsibility for her child's death? I began to see how many things in our society must be fundamentally wrong if women feel the imperative to make a choice like this.

What haunted me most were my patient's words, "I knew I couldn't handle that alone." They prompted me to reflect on how my parents had raised Iris. My mother had always had a husband at her side who would allow her, at times, to be weak and to need his help. Theirs was the kind of relationship my patient clearly lacked.

What's more, my parents had received support from a committed Christian community. Both of them had let go of their

"No Grumps Allowed!"
Iris recently drew this sign for the entry to *Plough*'s offices.

careers – my father as a civilian employee of the US Navy, my mother as the director of a kindergarten – to answer a calling to the Bruderhof, where they met and married. That's why, when Iris was born, they were surrounded by dozens of people who provided practical and emotional support, advice, and prayers. In the years that followed, these were the people who constantly helped us to see the beauty in Iris's life.

The Bruderhof community in upstate New York in which we grew up (and still live) is like a small village of about three hundred. Here Iris has always had friends her own age and has rarely felt excluded. Since high school, she has participated in the daily life of the community, doing activities suited to her abilities, such as setting tables in the communal dining room or helping in the community workshop, which makes adaptive equipment for other people with disabilities. Because communal living provides a wide diversity of tasks, it's never been hard to find her meaningful ways to contribute, even though in society at large she might not be capable of holding a paying job.

Members of the Bruderhof don't earn a salary or have their own bank account; by sharing our resources, income, skills, and workload, we seek to care for each other's needs. No one is concerned that a person like Iris might be consuming more than she contributes; each member is simply appreciated for the individual he or she is. If Iris gets sick, community members trained as doctors and nurses stand ready to care for her; others will take turns spelling off family members when we need a break. And although my parents do sometimes wonder what will become of Iris when they're gone, they know that she has community brothers and sisters who are as committed to her as her blood relations.

As I grieved for the mother in the Leipzig hospital and for her son, it dawned on me how much of my family's reality I had failed to see while growing up. Because Iris and others like her were so naturally integrated into every facet of our community's life, I had not registered how different her life would have been outside of this environment. For the first time, I saw clearly the scale of the challenges she lived with, challenges that elsewhere might have meant hired caregivers or a care home. I saw too the miracle of how, in a communal life, the gifts that Iris had to offer could be received. She was not only cared for; she was also able to reciprocate. Here, as perhaps nowhere else, she could blossom. "All my life," I thought, "the works of God have been sparkling before my eyes; it is I who have been blind."

In the weeks that followed, I realized that the horror of abortion was something in which I was implicated. I was living in accordance with the ideals of a society fixated on achievement and profit, a society with little room for those who will always be dependent – for people like Iris. In such a world, was it any wonder that a woman might feel she "couldn't handle that alone"? What hope could I offer her that her child would find a place where his gifts could be received, as Iris's have been? To be sure, from childhood on I'd known many dedicated families, therapists, and special needs teachers who shower their kids with love. Yet because their heroic efforts are made within a system so radically hostile to the weak, there are few happy endings. How could I credibly ask my patient to welcome a child with a disability unless I could also point her to a completely different way of living – one in which her son could flourish?

I experienced the truth of Oscar Wilde's words: "God's eternal Laws are kind and break the heart of stone. . . . How else but through a broken heart may Lord Christ enter in?" My heart of stone was broken and Christ entered in, in the form of that tiny, twenty-three-week-old boy. Recognizing that my creed of autonomy and success excluded those who could attain neither, I turned from it and eventually returned to the Bruderhof, where I became a member.

Today Iris and I still form an extended household with our parents. Living with her, I've had ample chances to see how a community that includes people of all abilities can be a healing balm for those of us who are sometimes prone to measure ourselves or others by false standards. Jean Vanier, the founder of the L'Arche community, describes it well:

> People with intellectual disabilities are not able to assume important roles of power and of efficacy. They are essentially people of the heart. When they meet others they do not have a hidden agenda for power or for success.

Their cry, their fundamental cry, is for a relationship, a meeting heart to heart. It is this meeting that awakens them, opens them up to life, and calls them forth to love in great simplicity, freedom, and openness.

When those ingrained in a culture of winning and of individual success really meet them, and enter into friendship with them, something amazing and wonderful happens. They too are opened up to love and even to God. They are changed at a very deep level. They are transformed and become more fundamentally human.[3]

> "People with intellectual disabilities are people of the heart."
>
> Jean Vanier

Such a community can be born whenever and wherever we open our hearts to one another's joys and sorrows and commit to sharing the load. Just as every human being is able to experience happiness, no human being is exempt from suffering. Even eminent scientists like Richard Dawkins suffer. In community, people like Iris can help the rest of us to bear our load. They can help us become more fundamentally human.

So I dream of the day when someone like Iris finds community with Richard Dawkins. I dream of the day when they become friends, two human beings equally endowed with life and love, yet carrying fears, hurts, and imperfections. I dream of the way they would be able share in each other's sufferings and joys; of the way both of their burdens could then become lighter. On that day, they together would come a little closer to reducing suffering and increasing the sum of happiness. ➤

1. Richard Dawkins, "Abortion and Down Syndrome," blog post, August 21, 2014 at *richarddawkins.net.*

2. Brian G. Skotko, Susan P. Levine, and Richard Goldstein, "Having a Son or Daughter with Down Syndrome: Perspectives from Mothers and Fathers"; "Having a Brother or Sister with Down Syndrome: Perspectives from Siblings"; and "Self-Perceptions from People with Down Syndrome" in *American Journal of Medical Genetics Part A,* October 2011, 155A(10):2335–2369.

3. Jean Vanier, acceptance speech for the 2015 Templeton Prize, March 11, 2015.

William H. Johnson, *Come to Me, Little Children*

*Image from Smithsonian American Art Museum*

# The Gospel of Life

*Readings from* Evangelium Vitae

**JOHN PAUL II**

*Twenty-one years ago, Pope John Paul II issued his apostolic letter* Evangelium Vitae, *addressing it to all people of good will. The pope's ringing condemnation of abortion and euthanasia, and his strictures on capital punishment, rightly captured broad attention. But his letter is far more than a list of moral rules. Today its prophetic proclamation of the whole gospel is more urgent than ever.*

THE GOSPEL OF LIFE is at the heart of Jesus' message. . . . This gospel has a profound and persuasive echo in the heart of every person – believer and nonbeliever alike – because it marvelously fulfills all the heart's expectations while infinitely surpassing them. . . .

The commandment "You shall not kill," even in its more positive aspects of respecting, loving, and promoting human life, is binding on every individual human being. It resounds in the moral conscience of everyone as an irrepressible echo of the original covenant of God the Creator with mankind. . . .

It is therefore a service of love which we are all committed to ensure to our neighbor, that his or her life may be always defended and promoted, especially when it is weak or threatened. It is not only a personal but a social concern which we must all foster: a concern to make unconditional respect for human life the foundation of a renewed society. . . .

Where life is involved, the service of charity must be profoundly consistent. It cannot tolerate bias and discrimination, for human life is sacred and inviolable at every stage and in every situation; it is an indivisible good. We need then to "show care" for all life and for the lives of everyone.

## False Freedom

The eclipse of the sense of God and of man inevitably leads to a practical materialism, which breeds individualism, utilitarianism, and hedonism. . . . The values of *being* are replaced by those of *having*. The only goal which counts is the pursuit of one's own material well-being. The so-called "quality of life" is interpreted primarily or exclusively as economic efficiency, inordinate consumerism, physical beauty and pleasure, to the neglect of the more profound dimensions – interpersonal, spiritual, and religious – of existence.

In such a context *suffering*, an inescapable burden of human existence but also a factor of possible personal growth, is "censored," rejected as useless, indeed opposed as an evil, always and in every way to be avoided. When it cannot be avoided and the prospect of even some future well-being vanishes, then life appears to have lost all meaning and the temptation grows in man to claim the right to suppress it.

In the materialistic perspective described so far, interpersonal relations are seriously impoverished. The first to be harmed are women, children, the sick or suffering, and the elderly. The criterion of personal dignity – which demands respect, generosity, and service – is replaced by the criterion of efficiency, functionality, and usefulness: others are considered not for what they "are," but for what they "have, do, and produce." This is the supremacy of the strong over the weak.

## The Role of Law

Although laws are not the only means of protecting human life, nevertheless they do play a very important and sometimes decisive role in influencing patterns of thought and behavior. I repeat once more that a law which violates an innocent person's natural right to life is unjust and, as such, is not valid as a law. For this reason I urgently appeal once more to all political leaders not to pass laws which, by disregarding the dignity of the person, undermine the very fabric of society. . . .

[Yet] it is not enough to remove unjust laws. The underlying causes of attacks on life have to be eliminated, especially by ensuring proper support for families and motherhood. A family policy must be the basis and driving force of all social policies. For this reason there need to be set in place social and political initiatives capable of guaranteeing conditions of true freedom of choice in matters of parenthood. It is also necessary to rethink labor, urban, residential, and social service policies so as to harmonize working schedules with time available for the family, so that it becomes effectively possible to take care of children and the elderly.

## Renewing Our Culture

What is urgently called for is a general mobilization of consciences and a united ethical effort to activate a great campaign in support of life. All together, we must build a new culture of life: new, because it will be able to confront and solve today's unprecedented problems affecting human life; new, because it will be adopted with deeper and more dynamic conviction by all Christians; new, because it will be capable of bringing about a serious and courageous cultural dialogue among all parties.

While the urgent need for such a cultural transformation is linked to the present historical situation, it is also rooted in the Church's mission of evangelization. The purpose of the gospel, in fact, is "to transform humanity from within and to make it new" (Paul VI, *Evangelii Nuntiandi*, 17). Like the yeast which leavens the whole measure of dough (Matt. 13:33), the gospel is meant to permeate all cultures and give them life from within, so that they may express the full truth about the human person and about human life. ⤳

---

*Taken from John Paul II, encyclical letter,* Evangelium Vitae *(March 25, 1995), 1, 77, 87, 90, 95.*

PETER MOMMSEN

# Building the Jesus Movement

## An Interview with Shane Claiborne

Many willing hands help construct a hydroponic greenhouse in the Simple Way park for local families in the Kensington neighborhood of Philadelphia. Today the greenhouse produces organic vegetables, while the watertank below houses fish whose waste serves as fertilizer.

**S**hane Claiborne, the well-known activist and author, wants "a Christianity that looks like Jesus." His Simple Way community in Philadelphia's Kensington neighborhood seeks to live out the revolutionary vision of the Sermon on the Mount: peacemaking, racial reconciliation, and a life rich in relationships instead of possessions.

*Plough* asked Shane what he's learned about communal living, how marriage has changed him, why millennials are leaving Christianity, and his newest mission: abolishing the death penalty.

**Peter***: Shane, you and I are speaking together outside the US Supreme Court building, where you're part of a four-day vigil calling for an end to capital punishment. That's also the focus of your latest book,* Executing Grace, *which argues that abolition should be a priority for US Christians. Why this issue now?*

**Shane:** When some people hear me say "death penalty" they go, "Ooh, sounds like debate class in high school!" I get that. But what sets this issue apart – what makes it so disturbing – is that we Christians are the biggest champions of executions in this country. In fact, the regions where the death penalty has flourished are precisely the areas where Christians are most concentrated. Eighty-five percent of all executions since 1976 have happened in the Bible belt. Other studies confirm that the group that supports capital punishment most fervently is evangelical Christians – much more so than secular people.

For followers of Jesus, other life issues, including abortion, remain very important.

But what's unique about the death penalty in the United States is that we Christians own it. Without our support, it probably would no longer exist.

*Why do Christians love the death penalty?*

There are many reasons. But the most troubling one stems from a fundamental misunderstanding of why Jesus died. Since I started talking about this issue, I have gotten emails from people asking, "How can God be against the death penalty when God used it to save humanity through Jesus' execution?" So Jesus' death is used as a reason to kill people.

*As you point out, the early Christians would have been appalled at that kind of thinking.*

The Christians of the first three centuries had a consistent ethic of life – they spoke out against all killing, without exception, including war, abortion, and the death penalty. They asked: Why do we call it murder when one person kills another in private life, but call it killing if it's done in war or through execution? Two thousand years ago they were already naming these contradictions.

An overwhelming majority of Americans actually know this. In a recent Pew poll that asked people whether Jesus would support the death penalty, only 5 percent said yes.

*Your book discusses the history of American racial violence, particularly of lynching. What's the link between this history and the death penalty today?*

A lot of the new research was initiated by Bryan Stevenson, a lawyer and founder of the Equal Justice Initiative in Alabama. He's found that it's exactly the places where lynchings were carried out a hundred years ago in which the death penalty flourishes today, in states like Texas, Georgia, Florida, and Alabama. Obviously, there's a complicated story here. Yet there does seem to be continuity between lynching – which, let's remember, often involved torture, mutilation, and burning in front of audiences of thousands – and what the Equal Justice Report calls "a more palatable form of violence" in the form of the death penalty after World War II. In 1950, African Americans made up 22 percent of the population but 75 percent of those executed. Today, African Americans are 12 percent of the population, yet make up 34 percent of folks executed and almost half (43 percent) of those on death row.

*Writers like Michelle Alexander and Ta-Nehisi Coates have highlighted the massive racial disparities in the US criminal justice system, which affect millions. Meanwhile, conservatives like Heather MacDonald point out that for young African-American males, the greatest risk of being killed is through violent crime. With these problems unresolved, is focusing on the death penalty a distraction?*

The death penalty is a gateway to talking about the broader issues of racial justice, because what's true for capital punishment is true for them too. For instance, statistically the biggest determinant for who gets executed is not the atrocity of the crime but the race of the victim. When the victim is white and the defendant is a person of color, he or she has a much higher chance first of being sentenced to death, and then of actually being executed.

**To learn more about the death penalty** in the United States and the movement to abolish it, read Shane Claiborne's book *Executing Grace: How the Death Penalty Killed Jesus and Why It's Killing Us* (HarperOne, 2016). For resources and links, visit *executinggrace.com*.

Shane with his wife, Katie Jo, who runs an afterschool program out of their home

One in three African-American boys born today can expect to go to prison. This has everything to do with our history: we haven't spoken the truth about slavery and racism, and we haven't done the necessary work of repentance and reconciliation. The United States accounts for 5 percent of the global population but 25 percent of the world's prisoners. There are more people of color in US prisons today than there were slaves in 1850. Slavery did not end, it just evolved.

These facts should cause us all to stop. In recent years, 156 folks have been released from death row after proving their innocence. In most cases, these exonerations only happened because of the work of students, volunteers, activists, and nonprofits. It's not the case that the criminal justice system is working.

*But don't the victims' families deserve justice too?*

Yes, and that is why I start my book by telling about the victims of violence. These murder victims' families are heroes of mine, people like SueZann Bosler. She and her dad, a pastor, were attacked by a church intruder who killed her father and almost killed her. At the trial, when given the chance to make a statement, she spoke against the death penalty. Despite the fact that she was the crime victim, the judge silenced her and actually threatened to hold her in contempt of court, with the chance of a fine or jail time. Voices like SueZann's are powerful in reminding us that violence is not the solution to violence. We've heard similar messages from families after the Boston Marathon bombing and the shooting at AME Emanuel Church in Charleston.

*You've called yourself pro-life from womb to tomb. What does that mean?*

Whenever we destroy life, we're working contrary to the Creator – we're squashing part of God's image in the world, as Cardinal Bernardin wrote back in 1982 when he called for a "consistent ethic of life." That means being pro-life from cradle to grave.

It's unhelpful that the term *pro-life* has come to mean only *anti-abortion*. In my neighborhood in Kensington, Philadelphia, to be pro-life means that I've got to figure out how to support a fifteen-year-old girl when she gets pregnant. These aren't just "issues," they're human beings.

That's why I love Mother Teresa so much. She used to say to young women in that situation, "If you don't know how to handle this, I'll help you." It's not just about picketing abortion clinics, it's about protecting life by supporting folks in really hard situations.

*On June 27, the US Supreme Court dramatically reaffirmed the constitutional right to abortion in the ruling* Whole Woman's Health v. Hellerstedt. *How should consistent pro-lifers respond?*

When I was in India in the 1990s working with Mother Teresa, I got to know two kids who were basically homeless. So I found a family in the United States who were ready to adopt them. When I asked Mother Teresa about it, though, she was adamant that she didn't want Indian kids going to the United States so long as our laws continued to make abortion so easy.

For those of us who are pro-life, the current state of affairs really puts a burden of responsibility on us to help bear the weight on people's shoulders. We need to be helping provide support groups for women who've had abortions and for women who are considering abortions. Because abortion has created a sort of national trauma.

## Being Bold for the Gospel

*Back in 2006, in your book* The Irresistible Revolution: Living as an Ordinary Radical, *you challenged Christians to "build a movement" inspired by the Sermon on the Mount. A decade later, are there signs of this movement taking shape?*

I see that everywhere – a movement of Christians who want Christianity to look like Jesus again, who want to be known not by what we're against but by what we're for. In the new 2016 edition of *The Irresistible Revolution,* I mention many amazing examples of where this stuff is happening, such as my friend Jeremy Courtney in Iraq with the Preemptive Love Coalition, or the folks with the Christian Community Development Association, which is now bigger than it has ever been.

There's evidence that folks are really longing for community. They're dissatisfied with a faith that means getting a ticket into heaven while ignoring the world around them, a faith that tells people, "Sorry your life sucks so much now. But you can look forward to life after death!" People ask, "Isn't there life *before* death?" They read the Sermon on the Mount and ask: What if Jesus really meant that? Here he tells us to love our enemies, so that probably means don't kill

> **We've got to love one person well – we can't just run programs.**

them. He says not to stockpile for tomorrow while people don't have enough for today – so what does that tell me about my 401(k) plan?

These questions challenge where our hope lies. As the old hymn goes, "My hope is built on nothing less than Jesus' blood and righteousness. . . . All other ground is sinking sand." There's a whole lot of sinking sand, and people are looking for something solid to stand on. What's beautiful is, we have Jesus as a cornerstone. The wisdom he offered two thousand years ago is just as relevant now as then. When he talks about unjust judges and widows and orphans and vineyard workers that don't get paid enough, he's talking about our world too.

*Are there parallels here to the Social Gospel movement in the last century? That movement eventually withered because it sidelined the importance of a personal relationship with Jesus.*

Too often we in the church separate things that were never meant to be separated. Faith and works have to work together like the two sides of scissors: loving God and loving neighbor are one command. Yes, we do pray, but we also get up off our knees and we go and we work for the things that God cares about.

We've got to learn to share about our faith in a way that's authentic and natural. Do you know the old saying that faith is less of a theory and more of a love affair? I love talking about my wife – so all the more I should love talking about my God and my Savior.

Recently, a friend of mine was talking with denominational leaders who were lamenting that the LGBT issue was going to dissolve their denomination. My friend pointed out that according to a recent study, the average

A Simple Way
community
house

member of their denomination only shared about Jesus with someone else once every five years. He told them, "Actually, if you're worried about your denomination, that's what you should be most worried about."

Folks today haven't grown up attending Sunday school or reading the Bible – it's new to them. We're seeing folks coming and saying, "I'm actually interested in reading the Bible. Tell me about Jesus."

Jesus tells us not to put our light under a bushel. Let's shine not for our sake, but because we're in love with God.

## Living in Community

*You and Katie Jo just celebrated your fifth wedding anniversary. How have those five years together changed you?*

Five years of marriage and we still like each other – we still love each other. It's funny because in some ways Katie's a lot more radical than me. When we got married, she said, "We don't need a microwave, and we don't need air conditioning. A lot of our neighbors don't have it, and it's kind of a privilege." So we got rid of our microwave and our air conditioning, even though Philadelphia can get to 105 degrees in summer. I've learned a trick: you can freeze one of those big water bottles and put it in your bed and it's your own personal air conditioner at night.

One thing I've learned from Katie is that we've got to love one person well – we can't just run programs. She had one young girl that needed a little extra help with school, and she took care of her six hours a day. Someone asked her, "Aren't there other kids that need help?" And Katie said, "Yes, and that's why *you're* here: to do for one person what you would want to do for everybody."

We got a tandem bike for our wedding and we rode off on that with the cans rattling behind! We still ride everywhere together.

*Your community, the Simple Way, started in 1997 as a communal household. What does it look like today?*

We originally moved in with ten people in a row house. Now it's evolved to about ten properties all in the same neighborhood of Kensington, and we're aiming to build a kind of village community. Over the years, as a community we've been through romanticism and then disenchantment. Now we're seeking about how to grow old together. How do we continue to love Jesus as passionately as when we were fifteen? And also: How do we get the dishes done? Who changes the oil in the car? We're still figuring that out.

*Are there any mistakes or mis-turns that others can learn from?*

We've made all kinds of wonderful mistakes over these twenty years. But one thing we did well from the beginning was to say, "We aren't choosing community, we're choosing each other." As Bonhoeffer said, we want not to be in love with our vision for community, but rather to love one another and the people around us. Community grows out of that.

When people come to the Simple Way thinking they're going to see fifteen people living together perfectly in this little drop of heaven on earth, yes, they're disappointed. But what's just as common is that people come away from visiting the Simple Way saying, "Wow, we can do this too! It's not that spectacular."

We've got our share of lumps and bruises. In the end, my interest isn't in people doing what the Simple Way does. My interest is that they should be who God made them to be and to find community in whatever form that takes.

> **Young people aren't leaving the church because we've made the gospel too hard but because we've made it too easy.**

Ultimately, that means to fall in love with Jesus.

*What day-to-day practices in communal living have become especially important to you?*

In our early years, we picked up some important tools by visiting your community, the Bruderhof. One tool we learned from you was to create a culture where confession comes naturally – to make a space for people to say "I'm sorry." The idea of confession and repentance is very countercultural in our world.

Another tool we learned from the Bruderhof is the importance of straight talk: being able to talk directly to each other as Jesus tells us to in Mathew 18. That's something we always have to keep getting back to. In his monastic rule, Saint Benedict warned against "murmuring," by which he meant talking negatively about each other, which creates an environment that's toxic for community.

Communities like ours and yours are really like cells of the body. Cells are born and cells die, but the body lives. The great thing about having a community of communities, a body with cells, is that we can help each other out. What we *do* have in common is a focus on Jesus and the Sermon on the Mount. That's the lens through which we can understand Scripture and understand the world that we live in.

## Past Church, Future Church

*Several newer Christian communities call themselves "new monastics," and the Simple Way has been called that as well. Are you a monastic?*

When we started a community and folks started calling it monasticism, I joked that some of my neighbors would be like, "I know you're kind of nasty, but *monasty?*" So "new

Mentoring neighborhood children is one of the Simple Way's main ministries.

monasticism" is not language that I use in my neighborhood necessarily.

But what is helpful about language is that it connects us to history and it gives us the humility to realize that what we're doing has been done before. The spirit of the desert monastics in the third and fourth centuries can help us. Sister Margaret, one of my mentors and an eighty-year-old Medical Mission sister, says that the inner city is the contemporary desert. It's where we go to find God and where demons and angels are at war. The Desert Fathers and Mothers loved God with a single-mindedness – that's where the *mono* of *monasticism* comes from.

Through the centuries, the purity of the gospel has often become so watered down by the narcissistic gospel of prosperity and by the war gospel. We who want the gospel of Jesus need examples from the past, and the monastic tradition is one of them. We have so much to learn from communities, like the Bruderhof, that have been around for generations and are still full of vitality. We can learn from the historic black church in this country, from Oscar Romero and the Jesuits in El Salvador,

from the civil rights movement, from John and Vera Mae Perkins. The more diverse our cloud of witnesses, the better off we are.

*We've spoken about history, but what about the future? Many Christians are worried about "the rise of the nones" – the growing number of young people who say they have no religious affiliation.*

I'm convinced that a lot of young people aren't leaving the church because we've made the gospel too hard but because we've made it too easy. We've thought that young people want to be entertained with louder worship music and fun youth nights with blow-up sumo dolls.

Now, young people might come for that, but they're not going to stay because of that. They'll stay because we've given them a vision for God's kingdom coming on earth. They'll stay because of a gospel that challenges them to dive into the deep darkness of our world where people have been forsaken. They'll stay because Jesus dares us to be as courageous for the cross as we've been for the sword. ⇥

*Interview by Peter Mommsen on June 30, 2016.*
▶ *Watch the interview at* plough.com/claiborne.

# Womb to Tomb

## Imagining a Completely Pro-Life Politics

**RONALD J. SIDER**

Whenever national elections roll around, many Christians ask how their faith should shape their politics. This year's US presidential election campaign has lent a charge of urgency to this perennial question. What's important for Christians to remember when they go to the polling booth – if they go at all?

The first thing to remember is that politics is secondary. For Christians, what's far more important is to simply be the church – to live out day by day what it means to be a faithful disciple of Jesus. The example of the Christian church of the first three centuries demonstrates how powerful and effective the church's mere existence can be, as we will see below.

All the same, it does not follow that Christians should withdraw from political engagement. This temptation can be powerful, especially this year, as we see how exceedingly nasty, vicious, dishonest, and depressing politics can become. As a result, many good Christians conclude that we should just turn our backs on the whole messy business.

That, I believe, is a mistake for two reasons: one practical, one theological.

In practical terms, history teaches that political decisions can have a huge impact for good or bad on the lives of billions. Think of

*Ronald J. Sider is president emeritus of Evangelicals for Social Action and a professor of theology and public policy at Palmer Theological Seminary of Eastern University.*

the devastation the world might have avoided if German Christian voters had voted differently in 1933. Think, by contrast, of the freedom that followed for tens of millions when the British evangelical politician William Wilberforce, after thirty years of lobbying, persuaded fellow members of parliament to outlaw first the slave trade, and then slavery itself, throughout the British Empire.

Today, it is through politics that we develop laws that either restrict or permit widespread abortion, protect or weaken religious liberty, harm or empower the poor, and conserve or destroy the environment. Politics is simply too important to ignore.

The theological reason for political engagement is even weightier. The central Christian confession is that Jesus is now Lord – Lord of the entire universe. The New Testament explicitly teaches that he is now "ruler of the kings of the earth" (Rev. 1:5). "All authority in heaven and on earth" has been given to the risen Jesus (Matt. 28:18). Christians who know that must submit every corner of their lives to this wonderful Lord.

Since we live in a democratic society where we have the freedom to vote, how we cast our ballot (or don't) shapes what happens to the communities in which we live. One way Christians must live out our belief that Christ is Lord, even of political life, is to think and pray for wisdom to act politically in ways that best reflect Christ our Lord.

But that raises the question: how do we let Christ be Lord of our politics? First, we must have a passion for truth. Christians know that God hates lies – and also that lying in politics is bad for democracy. So in this and every election season, Christians should insist on knowing the truth. Fact-checking organizations such as Politifact or Factcheck can help inform us whether what a politician says is accurate.

Pope Francis visits a refugee camp in Central African Republic (2015).

# An Unreserved Yes to Life

## Pope Francis

**The "culture of waste"** that today enslaves the hearts and minds of so many comes at a very high cost: it asks for the elimination of human beings, especially if they are physically or socially weaker. Our response to this mentality is a decisive and unreserved yes to life. . . . Things have a price and can be sold, but people have a dignity; they are worth more than things and are above price. . . .

In a frail human being, each one of us is invited to recognize the face of the Lord, who in his human flesh experienced the indifference and solitude to which we so often condemn the poorest of the poor, whether in developing countries or in wealthy societies. Every child who, rather than being born, is condemned unjustly to being aborted, bears the face of Jesus Christ, bears the face of the Lord, who even before he was born, and then just after birth, experienced the world's rejection. . . . And every elderly person, even if he is ill or at the end of his days, bears the face of Christ. They cannot be discarded, as the "culture of waste" suggests! They cannot be thrown away! ➤

Address to the International Federation of Catholic Medical Associations, Rome, September 20, 2013.

Second, Christians should have a passion for civility in the political arena. Biblical faith calls us to respect every person, no matter how much we disagree with him or her, because every person is both made in the image of God and loved by God. Civility reflects our reverence for the divine image in each person. It demands that we genuinely seek to understand those with whom we disagree. Christians should demand this virtue from all politicians, especially those who claim the Christian badge. At a minimum, this means protesting both racist innuendo and the encouragement of violence against opponents.

> **If we want to be biblically balanced in our politics, we cannot be one-issue voters.**

Third, in politics we must pursue a biblically balanced agenda. How can we discern what this agenda should be? I propose that the answer will come from asking a further question: What does the Bible say God cares about?

When we turn to the whole of Scripture, it quickly becomes clear that the God of the Bible cares about both the sanctity of human life and economic justice (especially for the poor); about both marriage and peacemaking; about sexual integrity, racial justice, and creation care. The political vision of the Bible is what I call "completely pro-life."

## Embracing Consistency

In January 2016 I spoke to a large evangelical conference held to coincide with the annual March for Life in Washington, DC, when thousands gather each year on the anniversary of the US Supreme Court's *Roe v. Wade* decision to call for an end to widespread abortion on demand. In my remarks, I recounted how for decades I've believed that Christians should act on a basic truth about the beginning of human

Photograph by Giovanni Portelli Photography

life: that from the moment of conception, we are dealing with persons made in the image of God. That's why I've joined in the movement to reduce abortion both by legislation and through supportive programs to assist unwed pregnant mothers.

While remaining committed to these goals, I've been disturbed by a fundamental inconsistency in much of the pro-life movement. People who are passionate about combating abortion often seem unconcerned about other ways that human lives are destroyed. Why, I wondered, did many pro-life leaders fail to support programs designed to reduce starvation among the world's children? Why did others oppose government funding for research into a cure for AIDS? Why did an important pro-life senator fight to save unborn babies only to defend government subsidies for tobacco products, which cause six million deaths around the globe each year? When Congressman Barney Frank quipped that pro-lifers believe that "life begins at conception and ends at birth," he was not being entirely unfair.

We in the pro-life movement can do better. Leaders such as Pope Francis have shown the way by calling on us to defend the sanctity of life consistently. In his speech to the US Congress in 2015, he said that Christian faith teaches "our responsibility to protect and defend human life at every stage of its development."

Global poverty, to take one example, is a pro-life issue: eighteen thousand children under five die every day, most from hunger or medically preventable causes. President George W. Bush launched, and President Obama continued, the PEPFAR program to combat treatable diseases such as malaria and AIDS. Yet despite millions of lives saved, major politicians have called for dramatic cuts in PEPFAR's funding. Shouldn't Christians be the

# Loving All Children – Both Unborn and Born

## Spencer Perkins

**Abortion – and the pro-life movement –** present black evangelicals with a dilemma. It is not that we question the evil of abortion; Jesus clearly would have condemned it. But for me, a black man, to join your demonstrations against abortion, I would need to know that you understand God's concern for justice everywhere. . . .

It is not a simple, glib response, then, when I must counsel an unwed black teenager against an abortion, even though I believe with all my heart that abortion is morally wrong. I feel that if the love of Christ compels me to save the lives of children, that same love should compel me to take more responsibility for them once they are born.

---

*Spencer Perkins, who helped his parents John and Vera Mae Perkins found Voice of Calvary Ministries, ran the magazine* Urban Family *and led Antioch Community, an integrated Christian community, until his death in 1998 at age forty-three.*

Quoted in Clark and Rakestraw, *Readings in Christian Ethics*, vol. 2, 268, 70.

first to support effective programs that prevent unnecessary deaths?

Environmental degradation is a pro-life issue. Global warming, unless we act soon, will cause devastating climate change that will lead to the deaths of millions of poor people.

Racism is a pro-life issue. In American history, white racism enabled the enslavement of tens of millions of Africans made in the image of God; after slavery ended, thousands of African-Americans were murdered in lynchings. Today, young black men are killed by police at far higher rates than young white men are.

Capital punishment is a pro-life issue. How can killing a person guilty of killing another person ever serve to teach respect for the sanctity of human life?

This list, of course, is far from complete. The point is, if we want to be biblically balanced in our politics, we cannot be one-issue voters. We must be pro-life and pro-poor, pro-family and pro-racial justice, pro-sexual integrity and pro-peace.

In real-life politics, we will find few, if any, viable candidates who fully represent the completely pro-life agenda. So we must weigh the various candidates' platforms (and likely actions) and then vote for the one closest to what the Bible teaches us God cares about. Sometimes, that means deciding for the candidate likely to do the least harm.

> In every age, the first, most important political act is to be the church.

## First-Century Pro-Lifers

To many Christians, this way of thinking about the sanctity of life – despite its profound rooting in scripture – may feel unfamiliar. How valuable, then, that we have access to the bracing pro-life witness of the New Testament's first readers: the early Christians. In my book, *The Early Church on Killing*, I collected every document and artifact I could find on the teaching and practice of the early church on killing up to AD 313, the year that Constantine legalized Christianity in the Roman Empire.

The consistency of the early church's pro-life convictions is astounding. Whether the issue is abortion, capital punishment, infanticide, or killing in war, every extant statement by Christian authors before Constantine says that Christians should never kill. The Christian writer Lactantius, writing in the early fourth century during the severe empire-wide persecution of Emperor Diocletian, sums up this consensus by flatly forbidding believers to serve in the military or participate in capital punishment: "Killing a human being is always wrong because it is God's will for man to be a sacred creature" (*Divine Institutes,* 6,20).

In accordance with the early Christian conviction that every human life is sacred, eight different authors in eleven different writings unanimously reject abortion. The blunt condemnation of the *Didache* is typical: "You shall not murder a child by abortion." In most instances, the writers condemn abortion either because the unborn child has a soul from the moment of conception or because abortion is killing and Christians do not do that. Thus Tertullian condemns abortion because Christians believe that all murder is wrong: "In our case, murder being once for all forbidden, we may not destroy even the fetus in the womb" (*Apology,* 9).

By the same token, four different writers say that Christians must not participate in capital punishment. *The Apostolic Tradition,* a church order probably from the late second or early third century, explicitly teaches that if a prominent government official (one who "wears red") authorized to order the death penalty asks to become a Christian, he must abandon his government position if he wants to become a candidate for baptism: "One who has the power of the sword or the head of a city and wears red, let him stop or be excluded."

The texts prohibiting killing in war are even more frequent. Up until the time of Constantine, there is not a single Christian writer known to us who says that it is legitimate for Christians to kill or to join the military; meanwhile, a substantial number of passages written over a period of many years explicitly say that Christians must not or do not kill or join the military:

- Nine different Christian writers in sixteen different treatises explicitly say that killing is wrong.

- Four writers in five treatises clearly argue that Christians do not and should not join the military. In addition four writers in eight different works strongly imply the same.

- At least eight times, five different authors apply the Messianic prophecy about swords being beaten into ploughshares (Isaiah 2:4) to Christ and his teaching.

- Ten different authors in at least twenty-eight different places cite or allude to Jesus' teaching to love your enemies, and in at least nine of these places, they connect that teaching to some statement about Christians being peaceful, ignorant of war, or opposed to attacking others.

It is also true that the documents show that by AD 173 there were a few Christians serving in the Roman army; their numbers increased substantially in the late third and early fourth centuries. But these Christian soldiers were doing what all extant statements on the topic by Christian authors clearly condemned.

In summary, early church history confirms what a biblically balanced approach urges: a completely pro-life agenda.

## Putting It into Practice

How do we apply this early Christian vision today? Partly, of course, our historical context will influence our response. All the same, in every age, the first, most important political act

Friedrich Wilhelm Schadow,
*The Wise and Foolish Virgins* (detail)

## The Early Christian Witness

From the *Didache* (ca. AD 60–110)

**There are two ways,** one of life and one of death, and there is a great difference between these two ways.

Now this is the way of life: First, you shall love God, who made you. Second, you shall love your neighbor as yourself; but whatever you do not wish to happen to you, do not do to another. The teaching of these words is this: Bless those who curse you, and pray for your enemies, and fast for those who persecute you. For what credit is it if you love those who love you? Do not even the Gentiles do the same? But you must love those who hate you, and you will not have an enemy. . . .

The second commandment of the teaching is: You shall not murder; you shall not commit adultery; you shall not corrupt children; you shall not be sexually immoral; you shall not steal; you shall not practice magic; you shall not engage in sorcery; you shall not abort a child or commit infanticide. . . . You shall not hatch evil plots against your neighbor. You shall not hate anyone; instead you shall reprove some, and pray for some, and some you shall love more than your own life. ⇥

*Didache* 1.1–4, 2.1–7, trans. Michael W. Holmes in *Apostolic Fathers* (Baker Academic, 2007).

is to be the church – to live out in community the full implementation of Jesus' kingdom teaching. That is what the early church sought to do. They did it even though very few Christians were Roman citizens and the empire frequently persecuted and sometimes killed them. No matter what the external political setting, the church should be the church.

The early church lived out their refusal to kill in striking ways that eventually revolutionized society. Abortion and infanticide were widespread but the early church rejected both; in time, both became far rarer. Gladiatorial contests, too, first declined in importance and then were banned as a result of the Christians' refusal to even attend this once-popular "sport." Slowly and bit by bit, the Christian church's pro-life vision affected the wider culture in profound ways.

> I do not believe God has one ethic for Christians and another for the world.

The same has happened again and again throughout history – whenever Christians have modeled a new way of living in the church, their example has changed the surrounding society. Hospitals and schools for poor children started because Christians felt compelled by Christ's love to care for the sick and to educate poor children; eventually, the larger society agreed that everyone should have health care and education. The sixteenth-century Anabaptists insisted that the church should be a believers' church free of state control and eventually – after thousands were martyred – governments made religious liberty a constitutional right. Today, if the body of Christ becomes a living model of racial embrace, peacemaking, and economic justice for the poor, we will reshape our societies.

To what extent should Christians try to persuade the secular world to live according to the completely pro-life vision of the gospel? We must start by candidly recognizing that non-Christians will never be able to fully live the way Jesus taught. The Christian has three things the non-Christian does not have: the powerful, supernatural presence of the Holy Spirit empowering us to live like Christ; the liberating power that comes from knowing our sins are forgiven and we are accepted by God in spite of our sin; and finally, the strong support of a Christian community. Thus, Christians cannot expect non-Christians to always live like Jesus.

And yet: they *should* live like him. I do not believe God has one ethic for Christians and another for the world. God wants all people to love their enemies and refuse to kill.

Paul tells us in the first two chapters of Romans that the law of God is written on the heart of everyone (see especially 2:14–15). When Christians consistently proclaim biblical truths about the sanctity of human life and about justice for the poor, even non-Christians will sense that this message is true and right.

If Christians articulate a completely pro-life agenda boldly – through our words, in our daily lives, and in the voting booth – many people in the larger society will respond. When we do this, it will be an act of love toward the billions of our neighbors who will be helped. And it will serve to proclaim that Jesus, who came to bring abundant life (John 10:10), truly is Lord over all the world. ➤

---

*For further reading, see the author's books* Just Politics: A Guide for Christian Engagement *(Brazos, 2012) and* The Early Church on Killing: A Comprehensive Sourcebook on War, Abortion and Capital Punishment *(Baker, 2012).*

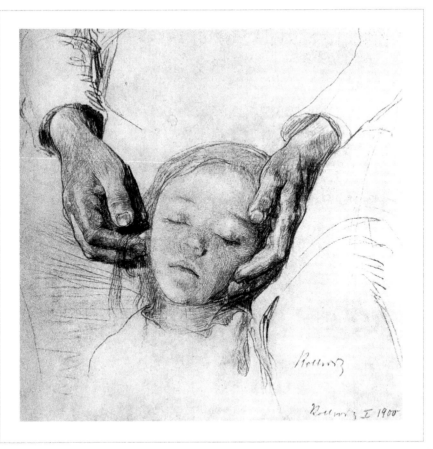

Käthe Kollwitz, *Untitled*

# A World Where Abortion Is Unthinkable

**SHELLEY DOUGLASS**

I have four kids. Two of them I bore myself, and two are adopted. I realized, not too long ago, that even the two I bore would today be good candidates for abortion. Paul, who's the oldest, was conceived almost on my wedding night, when I was still an undergraduate. He did make it hard to finish my degree, I'll have to admit, but there was never any question of not having this child. Thomas, born about four or five years later, came along right after the legalization of abortion. At the time I was pregnant with him I was in the middle of a marriage breakup, living at a Catholic Worker house, with an income of about

*Shelley Douglass is a Catholic peace activist. With her husband, James W. Douglass, she founded the Ground Zero Center for Nonviolent Action in Poulsbo, Washington, and Mary's House, a Catholic Worker house in Birmingham, Alabama. A version of this article appeared in* Harmony: Voices for a Just Future, *vol. 2 no. 3.*

$50 a month, and with another of the children living with me. There was strong pressure from the people in the Catholic Worker house for me to have an abortion. That's not typical for Catholic Workers, but it's what happened to me. It really wasn't something that I seriously considered, because I wanted to have the child. But when I thought about it later I realized that both of those children would have been candidates for abortion today.

Having participated in several feminist support groups, I've had a fair amount of experience with discussion of abortion, as many of us have.

One of the most telling experiences happened in King County Jail in Seattle. A valuable thing about going to jail is that you meet people you'd never meet otherwise. In this particular instance, I was in jail for taking part in anti-nuclear actions of civil disobedience with eight other activists, all of us white. Everyone else in the jail was either black, Native American, or Hispanic; there were maybe seventy of us all told.

When you're in jail, you do anything to get out of your cell – it's boring in that cell! There was a women's health collective that came in every two weeks to do education on health care for the prisoners; you could go or not, whatever you wanted to do. We always went, because at least it was a change of scene and something different to talk about.

One day we walked in and the presentation was on abortion. The two women who came in clearly believed what they were saying and felt that they were bringing something that would

It's hard to imagine the kind of justice that would have to exist for there really to be a world where abortion is unthinkable. Not illegal: unthinkable!

make life better. There's no question – they were not out to do these women in. They had no financial interest that I know of in any decision these women might make. They really did want to share that abortions were normal, an easy thing, a very simple thing to do, that you really ought to consider it, especially if you were financially embarrassed. Everyone in jail is, of course. After the two women explained about abortion there was a silence. Then one of the women from the streets said, "But why would I want to kill my baby?"

The answer was, "Well, it's not really a baby yet. It's not a big thing – you might as well do this because then you won't have little children to support." One of the visitors finally said, "Well, you know, it's simple: I got pregnant when I was writing my thesis and I just couldn't do both, so I had an abortion, and it was fine, and I got my thesis in."

What I remember about that conversation is the total puzzlement of the women in jail; there was a complete cultural divide, no meeting at all. And there is truth on both sides: there is an economic pressure that makes it very hard for people to bear children, especially people in the ghetto who have no option to get out. (Most of the women we were with were prostitutes.) There was definitely the truth of economic reality; on the other hand, there was a very instantaneous human response: Why would I want to kill my baby?

For me those truths sum up two important things: that society is evil, or fallen, or sinful, and it creates a struggle between the mother and the unborn, so the mother feels she must abort in order to survive. There is also a very basic truth in the assumption that the unborn is a developing child, and why would we want to kill it?

That leaves me with a lot of questions: What is it we're trying to do? What are we working for, and where do we want to go with all this? Where do we want to end up when we're done?

I've had some answers that are really visions. One is that we're trying to create a new world – and there are a number of kinds of worlds that can be created by people's energies. I'm aware that when I imagine a world where abortion is unthinkable, it isn't necessarily what other people think of. I need to be specific when I say, "a world where abortion is unthinkable." *Why* is abortion unthinkable; what makes it that way? I've met people who were projecting a world where abortion is unthinkable because we were so regimented and women were so oppressed into being breeders that there was no freedom; all children would be carried to term, and there were no other ways to decide. That's not what I mean when I think of a world where abortion isn't considered.

What I think of is a world where all people, all humankind, are valued just because they're human, where they're welcome just because they're human. A world of generosity. I think of Catholic Worker homes, where there is always room to pull up another chair to the table, always a little more to go around, a world where there is welcome for people.

It would be a world of responsibility, where we think about what we're doing and take the consequences of our actions. A world of peace, where it's assumed that everybody will be sustained at a basic level, not a world where some people will be floating in superfluous wealth and other people starving. A peaceful world, where there are other ways of solving conflicts than killing each other, a world where rape is also unthinkable, and where economics do not force women into sexual activity.

I think, if we were able to create a world where those were the assumptions, it would go a long way toward making a world where abortion wouldn't happen; it wouldn't be in the picture and it wouldn't be necessary. Martin Luther King Jr. talked about the "beloved community." That's the kind of world we work for, where everybody is beloved. He talked about a world where black children and white children, Gentiles and Jews, Protestants and Catholics – and so on – everybody, all the children, could play together and work together and have enough to eat and be respected.

It's hard to imagine the kind of justice, economic justice and justice for women, that would have to exist for there really to be a world where abortion is unthinkable. Not illegal: unthinkable! It's a spiritual question. It's as though our souls would have to be pulled out of our bodies and remade and put back in; we would need to change our heart of stone for a heart of flesh. When I'm talking about such a world, I'm a little bit shaky, because I know that somewhere deep inside there's that one thing I don't want to change, that I don't want to give up, and I'm not sure what it is. But I know it's there. It's that one thing I have to fight and learn to give up before the new world can come to be.

One of the guidelines for nonviolence is that if you want to go someplace, you have to "go by getting there." If you want the world to be one way, you have to live that way, and that helps the world become that way. Imagine a world where war and abortion are both unthinkable, and then start to live as if we already lived in that world – that moves us along the path. ⌖

Photo by Béatrice de Géa

**SAM HINE**

# Gardening with Guns

In a fresh take on "swords into plowshares," gun owners forge a creative alternative to murder, suicide, and fear.

**G**uns are tools, right? Police and soldiers use them to do their jobs, and many citizens feel safer with one strapped on. In the United States, the only country with more guns than people, it's no surprise that these weapons feature daily in the news: from terror attacks and mass shootings to the less publicized but more widespread epidemics of handgun violence, suicide, and accidental shootings by children.

## Turn War Around

The Second Amendment enshrines a distinctly American – and, some would say, sacred – freedom: the right to bear arms. How to reconcile that with the need to curb gun violence? Michael Martin, a young Mennonite from Colorado Springs, decided the best way to approach this emotionally charged issue was to tell a different story – to counter the debilitating stream of tragic news with an alternative narrative of transformation and restoration, one tool at a time.

Martin won't take away your rights, but if you happen to have a gun you want to be rid of, he'll be happy to forge it into a garden tool for you.

The idea hatched back in 2009 as Martin watched news coverage of the christening of the USS New York, a battleship with a bow stem made of steel from the fallen World Trade Center. ("Notice how they bring Christ into it.") Someone needed to counteract this rhetoric and symbolism of revenge, Martin felt. A big fan of Walter Brueggemann's approach to the Old Testament, he latched onto Isaiah's words, "They shall beat their swords into plowshares and their spears into pruning hooks." The prophet Micah repeats this refrain and adds, "They shall all sit under their own vines and under their own fig trees, and no one shall make them afraid." So, repurposing weapons to grow food as a way to drive out fear. "That's our end goal: to get to the point where we're not afraid of each other anymore."

It wasn't until Adam Lanza opened fire at Sandy Hook Elementary School in 2012, killing twenty children and six adults, that Martin knew he needed to act. His wife, Hannah, suggested they call their project RAWtools. ("You get RAW when you turn WAR around.") "Alongside the destructive narratives that the guns come out of, we want to share the creation narratives that have been born out of those – stories and pictures of the beautiful gardens and food being grown with the tools."

World Trade Center steel is forged into a warship.

*Sam Hine is an editor at Plough.*

### Thank God I'm Free

Mike Warren, a sixty-four-year-old former infantry soldier, provided the first weapon: an AK-47 assault rifle he acquired in the days after the September 11 terror attacks. "I was afraid," he admitted. According to the *Colorado Springs Gazette*, Warren, a sportsman who says he has no plans to dispose of his hunting guns, said the last straw for his assault rifle was the massacre at Sandy Hook. Warren's weapon was cut in half with an angle grinder. Holding the severed assault rifle high in the air, he said, "Thank God I'm free of the damn thing." Warren said he did not want to make a political statement: "I speak for nobody but myself."

A local rancher, Terry Brown, taught Martin and his father, Fred, to form the barrel into hand cultivators. Brown owns about thirty guns, which he says he needs to do his job – "to put an injured horse out of its misery, for example." Still, he thinks RAWtools is a good idea, and says he would never point a gun at another human being. "That's where I draw the line. Animals, yes; people, no." ∎

**For My Son**   Cherie Ryans lost her eighteen-year-old son Terence, a college student studying criminal justice, when bullets intended for someone else struck him as he left a movie theater in Philadelphia. Fifteen years later, RAWtools set up their anvil in the city and invited parents who had lost children to gun violence to beat on the barrel of a handgun *(right)* that had been removed from the streets. As tears streamed down her face, Ryans said slowly and forcefully, pounding the red-hot metal after every word, "This – is – for – my – son."

Martin says, "It really helped her release in a physical way a lot of the anguish that she dealt with. It helped us see what he meant to her, but also that fifteen years removed from

the incident, there was still deep, deep pain." Martin finds that women, especially mothers, are leading the movement to end gun violence: "They want to heal the world."

The tool, with a small hoe on one side and a two-prong tilling fork on the other, has been used to plant flowers for victims of gun violence in the Philadelphia area. ▪

*At right,* Terri Roberts takes a hammer to the barrel of a gun during a RAWtools demonstration.

## Their Love Melted Me

Perpetrators' families also suffer from gun violence. Terri Roberts is the mother of Charles Roberts IV, who ten years ago took Amish schoolgirls hostage in their one-room schoolhouse in Nickel Mines, Pennsylvania. He shot eight of the girls, killing five, before turning the gun on himself.

Within twenty-four hours the Amish families were at Terri's door, reaching out to her and her husband. Their love melted her. Over the years since the shooting, Terri has continued to develop a relationship with the victims' families. Every other Thursday, she visits one of the survivors, Rosanna, who still uses a wheelchair and eats with a feeding tube. Terri helps Rosanna bathe and reads or sings

with her. Spending time together has helped both of them heal. Every time Terri visits, she is confronted with the damage her son caused. But she is also reminded that violence need not have the last word. Terri recounts her journey in a book titled *Forgiven.* ■

## I Wanted to Die

Eleven years ago, a twenty-seven-year-old unemployed military veteran named Benjamin L. Corey was "broke, alone, divorcing, and about as clinically depressed as a person could get." He saw no reason to go on living, so he loaded his Smith & Wesson .22 and tried to work up courage to pull the trigger. On a quick run to the store to "grab something to drink and take the edge off before coming home to finish the job once and for all," he silently told God, "If you really love me, I need to know right now." In the store, a passing stranger put a note in his hand that saved his life (a story he recounts in detail on his Patheos blog).

Last summer Corey planted a garden with a tool made from his .22.

It is a Fact That God Loves You

"For God so loved the world, that He gave His only begotten Son, that whoever believes in Him should not perish, but have eternal life.

JOHN 3:16

The note that saved Benjamin Corey's life

Suicide accounts for more than 60 percent of gun violence, and about 85 percent of those deaths are white males. Afterward, the family is often left wondering what to do with the gun. When Kevin Wilder was eight years old, his father shot himself. Forty years later, Wilder donated the gun to RAWtools. "I've had the gun all this time," he said. "I couldn't give it to somebody else."

Photograph courtesy Benjamin L. Corey

Photograph Jerilee Bennett © Colorado Springs Gazette

Corey also donated the World War II Mauser pictured above. At right, he helps RAW-tools repurpose Kevin Wilder's gun, as shooting survivor David Works looks on. In 2007 Works and his family were shot in the parking lot of New Life Church in Colorado Springs. "To make a long story short, I started the day with four kids and I ended it with two." The gunman sprayed the family's minivan with bullets, killing teenage daughters Stephanie and Rachel. Less than a month later, the church's pastor asked Works and his wife Marie if they would be willing to meet the parents of the man who shot their daughters. The families met and have stayed in touch. ∎

## Vegetables for Young Offenders

"Why do our kids pick up sticks and turn them into guns?" Martin asks. "We've got a lot of work to do: when two-year-olds pretend a stick is a gun, we know that our imaginations have gone down the wrong road. Why can't they use the sticks to make a teepee or something?"

La Plazita Institute in Albuquerque draws on Native American practices and culture to help at-risk Native American and Latino youth, many of whom have already been in gangs and jail. This summer RAWtools helped the youth convert guns confiscated by Albuquerque police into garden tools. The youth are now using the tools in organic gardens that supply local public schools and the detention centers that house many of the young gardeners' peers.

"It's a beautiful full circle of reconciliation and reintegration and restoration," says Martin. "That's what we're about." ∎

**What's Next?**   Martin wants to try melting the aluminum in guns to form knitting needles, which will be used to empower women in Afghanistan to earn their living. He'd also like to see affiliates in every state, because of the restrictions on shipping guns across state lines.

"But converting guns has been the easy part," he says. "The hard part is the human element and changing the way we deal with conflict. Turning guns into garden tools points us to what we need to do with ourselves; it compels us to use our imaginations to look at the other tools that are out there, like mediation, talking circles, restorative justice, and anti-bullying programs.

"I see us as that hot metal: if we allow ourselves to be vulnerable to the heat of confrontation, then the cold steel of the anvil and the hammer – the work of the community and the work of the Spirit – can shape us. It's the hot steel – or the hothead – that is at its most impressionable, so when we have cool voices around us, or maybe the whisper of the Spirit, that can help shape us into better witnesses to Christ." ⇥

▶ *Watch RAWtools beat on guns and explain why they do at* plough.com/rawtools. *To donate guns or purchase tools, see rawtools.org. For more on Americans' devotion to guns, read* America and Its Guns: A Theological Exposé, *by James E. Atwood (Wipf & Stock, 2012).*

# A Good Death

*A nurse reflects on euthanasia, medicine, and the wisdom of being a burden.*

**STEVEN FOUCH**

Curled up on a chaise longue that had been adapted into a daybed, Bill was obviously not at peace. Pale and drawn, he moved slowly, grimacing, with the occasional twitch and jump in his limbs. As a community health nurse working in London for a Christian charity that ministers to AIDS patients, I had seen these symptoms before.

"How long has he been like this?" I asked Ian, a bespectacled man in his mid-thirties

Deidre Scherer, *Late May,* thread on fabric, 15 x 13"

*Steven Fouch, after years working as a community nurse in London, now works with the Christian Medical Fellowship in the British Isles as a speaker and writer on spiritual, ethical, and professional issues in nursing and healthcare.*

who had introduced himself as Bill's partner.

"For the last couple of hours, really. More or less since he got home," Ian replied, his anxiety and weariness barely disguised. "Can you do anything for him?"

There was plenty of reason for worry. Bill, who had an AIDS-related lymphoma, had just been discharged from a hospital where he had been admitted for a type of pneumonia common among AIDS patients at the time. The hard truth of the situation was that he had come home to die.

Ian told me that he and Bill had lived together for about ten years. Both worked in the media and had enjoyed successful careers. When Bill had been diagnosed as HIV-positive eight years earlier, they had coped and even thrived for a while. But once Bill developed AIDS-related illnesses, his freelance work had dried up, and Ian had had to be both caretaker and sole breadwinner. Those friends who had not dropped out of contact mostly lived too far away to lend anything more than moral support, while both their families wanted nothing to do with them.

Two hours later, I had set up a new diamorphine pump that would help Bill settle for the night and grant Ian a few hours' sleep. Bill smiled as he held my hand and said thanks. Ian hugged me grimly and wordlessly as I left.

The next day I came by in the late morning to check that they were OK. Bill had slept through the night and appeared less drawn. Ian also seemed more rested, but I sensed that he was not at ease. As I set up a new syringe driver in the kitchen, he came in and gently shut the door so Bill could not hear. "Is he going to get more like he was yesterday evening?" Ian asked.

"As long as we can keep his symptom relief working, he will be comfortable," I replied. "But he is going to get steadily weaker – I don't think he is going to make any significant recovery from this illness."

Ian drew a ragged breath. "Can you give him all the morphine in one go?"

"That would suppress his breathing and he could die," I replied, suspecting what was coming next.

"I don't want him to suffer. Can't you just . . . you know, fix it . . . so he drifts off peacefully?"

## The Final Moment

I have cared for many men and women at the end of their lives, and try as I might, not all of my patients have had what one could call "a good death." Some things are just out of one's control. But I do know that not one of my patients suffered for want of good care. I knew lots of Bills who had poorly planned discharges and who needed lots of extra support when they got home.

I experienced this firsthand with my own mother. She was discharged from hospice with no one at home to care for her. My sister had to drop everything to travel over a hundred miles to Mum's house. Within hours my sister was on the telephone begging me to come and help her after Mum fell while trying to get off the toilet.

My mother's condition nosedived, so I relocated my very young family and my work for the next six weeks as we cared for her in her last days. The support we got from friends, family, her doctor, and community nurses made all the difference. As a result, my mother ended her days seeing her granddaughter taking her first steps. My father-in-law, an Anglican minister, visited so that she could share communion and worship from her sickbed one last time with her family. She died surrounded by her children, family, and friends in the bedroom she had shared with my father, who had died two years earlier, in the house in which she had been born seventy-two years earlier. It was what I would call a good death.

For Bill and my mother, having the people they loved at hand was the "symptom control" they most wanted. I could set up diamorphine syringes to take the pain and nausea away, turn them regularly to avoid pressure sores, and feed them food they could tolerate and enjoy. All this is essential, basic, and good nursing care. But it was having the people they loved nearby, and sensing that their own lives still had meaning and value, that really made the difference. For my mother, ending her days in the knowledge that she was going to be with her Lord brought tremendous comfort.

I cared for Bill for only a few more days before he died naturally. Ian soon saw that Bill was comfortable, and that what he wanted more than anything was to say goodbye to those closest to him. Bill's family finally came to visit, as did many of his dearest friends, and his dying days were not spent in isolation.

When I saw Ian after the funeral, he admitted that if I had let him have his way that Saturday morning, overdosing Bill with diamorphine, this would have denied Bill the chance to say goodbye. It was a better end than Ian had feared, and in the midst of his grief he had the satisfaction of knowing that Bill had died knowing he was loved.

Most of the distress people experience at the end of life is ultimately spiritual: that sense of being lost, isolated, fearful, and unsupported; the fear of being a burden on your loved ones, and of uncontrolled symptoms; the grief that your entire life, with all your loves, your hopes, fears, dreams, and ambitions has come down to this small room, this bed where you are going to end your days. And possibly above all, there is the fear about what comes next – oblivion?

Some kind of afterlife? In a post-Christian West, there are no longer any accepted answers or structures to help people contend with these questions.

### The Burden of Being Human

Around the world, various groups are calling to make it legal to help end someone's life in the case of terminal illness. As a nurse who has worked with the dying, I sympathize with the natural desire to avoid unnecessary suffering at the end of life; it's the same impulse that undergirds palliative care and the hospice movement.

There is, however, a spiritual despair at the heart of this call for assisted dying. In a society that celebrates youth, vitality, beauty, and self-determination above all else, the fear of losing these is almost intolerable. Then only despair remains. One's last act of self-determination becomes to end one's own existence while one still has the autonomy to do so.

How different is the Christian understanding of the self. Scripture teaches us that we are not our own: we are Christ's (1 Cor. 6:19–20). As such, our lives are hugely valuable. It is not for us or anyone else to determine the timing and nature of our deaths.

Furthermore, we are not autonomous individuals, but part of a community, an interdependent body (1 Cor. 12:12–13). When one part suffers, all parts suffer. When one part rejoices, all rejoice. This is a community where we are enjoined to "bear one another's burdens."

Data published by Oregon's assisted suicide program over the last decade shows that the vast majority of patients cite the fear of being a burden as one of their main reasons for ending their lives early, alongside fear of loss of control

*We are meant to be burdensome to one another.*

Deidre
Scherer,
*Huddle*,
thread on
fabric,
34 x 34"

and independence and the feeling that life has
lost meaning and joy. [1]

Yet scripture tells us that we are meant to be
burdensome to one another
(Gal. 6:2). I was a burden to
my mother at the start of my
life. I saw this as I cared for
her and my eight-month-old
daughter at the same time.
I had to feed both of them,
change their diapers when
they soiled themselves, soothe
them to sleep when they were
distressed. My mother had done all of this for
me, and now I was doing it for her. There was a
natural symmetry. And while I wish my mother
had had many more years of life, I would not
have given up the chance to be with her and
care for her in those final weeks. It was one of

*The artist Deidre Scherer is a
pioneer in her medium of thread-
on-layered-fabric. She has created
two narrative series – *The Last
Year *and* Surrounded by Family
& Friends *– that promote an open
dialogue about aging and dying
as a natural part of life. Visit*
dscherer.com.

the most profound privileges of my life.

This mutual burdensomeness is part of
what makes us human. God himself shares in
this – bearing our sins and
suffering on the cross (Isa.
53:3–5). The Incarnation
reveals another depth of
human existence, for as Jesus
was once a helpless baby,
needing to be fed, washed,
and changed, so he was also
a dying man who needed
care and company in his
final hours. In taking on our humanity, God
endowed every helpless baby and every dying
person with the same value and dignity. In
caring for our children and the dying, we care
also for him (Matt. 25:35–40). It is one of the
most remarkable wonders and mysteries of the

Christian faith, and it is an experience that transformed me as both a nurse and a father.

## Daring Peace

When advocates for assisted dying argue that it is a lack of compassion that drives caretakers like me to oppose their agenda, we have had to constantly, compassionately, and patiently argue back with the facts. People do not need to die in pain and with uncontrolled symptoms. Allowing doctors or nurses to kill certain groups of people, or to assist them in killing themselves, will eventually lead to opening the same "option" to anyone who feels that his or her life is not worth living. We are already seeing this happen in the Netherlands and Belgium, where voluntary euthanasia legislation has slowly been extended to those with dementia, to those in comas, to infants and children, and most recently to those struggling with past traumas, anxious about the future, or simply tired of living. [2]

The consequences of removing these legal constraints are far-reaching. The vulnerable feel pressure (real or imagined) to stop burdening their families and society by ending their lives. Governments, healthcare systems, and insurance companies faced with mounting costs start to see assisted death as a cheaper, more "humane" alternative to long-term care. The symmetry of mutual burdensomeness is lost, and society loses its soul as it kills off those it deems unworthy of life in the name of autonomy and compassion.

Dietrich Bonhoeffer wrote, "There is no way to peace along the way of safety." Some of my colleagues have been vilified in the press and social media for taking stands against euthanasia. Yet time and again, our arguments have won over our legislators, much of the serious press, and healthcare professionals.

I well remember the look on the face of my CEO here at the Christian Medical Fellowship when, after having successfully helped to defeat two assisted-dying bills before the Westminster and Scottish parliaments, he received a call that another, newly re-elected MP would be bringing yet another bill before the House of Commons after the British general election in May 2015. Just as we thought the battle was won, the war began again. Fortunately, the bill went nowhere. After long and serious debate, with great speeches on both sides, the house overwhelmingly voted down the proposed legislation by a three-to-one majority, stalling this push in Westminster Parliament for at least the next five years.

To care and show compassion is an essential mark of discipleship (2 Cor. 1:3–7). Equally, discipleship demands the willingness to stand up and speak for truth, for the vulnerable, and for the marginalized (Isa. 1:17). As a nurse and as a Christian, I must do both. I cannot credibly do one without the other.

To give the best care, to enter into the world of the dying and their loved ones, to share those last days and help them have peace, to give comfort and meaning through those days – these are great privileges and responsibilities. But by that same token, we must work to ensure that the dying are not encouraged to prematurely terminate their lives in the mistaken belief that they are escaping suffering. Rather, it's our task to make sure they know that they, far from being unwanted burdens, are valued and loved to the end. ⤳

1. Oregon Death with Dignity Act: 2015 data summary, page 4; Oregon Public Health Division, February 4, 2016.

2. Scott Y. H. Kim; Raymond G. De Vries; John R. Peteet, "Euthanasia and Assisted Suicide of Patients with Psychiatric Disorders in the Netherlands 2011 to 2014," *JAMA Psychiatry* 73, no. 4 (2016): 362–368. See also Steve Doughty, "Sex Abuse Victim in Her 20s Allowed to Choose Euthanasia in Holland after Doctors Decided Her Post-traumatic Stress and Other Conditions Were Incurable," *Daily Mail,* May 10, 2016.

"What are the God-given talents of a pig? Unlike any other animal, it has a plow on its nose."

# Behold the Glory of Pigs

## JOEL SALATIN

A self-described "Christian, libertarian, environmentalist, capitalist, lunatic farmer," Joel Salatin raises pastured beef cows, pigs, turkeys, and laying hens on a family farm in Virginia's Shenandoah Valley.

Growing up in a conservative Christian family in rural Virginia, I witnessed more than a few conversations with churchgoing friends who could never understand why our family embraced health food, compost piles, and our dope-smoking hippie friends. In our home, there was nothing contradictory about being both a pro-life Christian and a good steward of our planet. But in recent years, it has become increasingly difficult to be accepted as someone who identifies as both.

planets. The Christian crowd, laughing and clapping, thought it was a great broadside against the pagans.

When progressive environmentalists advocate abortion while simultaneously risking life and limb to protect trees and whales, the Christian community indignantly calls out the unspeakable hypocrisy. Rightly so: after all, we're talking about ripping a thinking, feeling, hearing, reponding baby from the womb. But the charge of hypocrisy cuts both ways. Why are we Christians eating Happy Meals that come from chickens raised in despicable CAFOs (confinement animal feeding operations) on our way to the sanctity-of-life rally?

Dr. Francis Schaeffer, the great Christian philosopher, famously asked: "How shall we then live?" If Christians actually embraced an ethic of creation stewardship, we would own the moral high ground. Our testimony to the gospel of life would become far more credible once our actions began to bear out what we say we believe. However, when Christians cavalierly embrace the mechanistic view of life instead of seeing it as the sacred handiwork of the Creator, we lower ourselves to the egocentricity of a godless culture.

The result of this failure is that environmentalists are the pioneers in earth stewardship while the Christian community has earned the dubious distinction of conquistador, pillager, rapist, and earth destroyer. This segregated and hypocritical thinking does not serve the gospel. Christians have latched onto a misunderstood version of the "dominion" mandate of Genesis 1, failing to realize that this scripture is really a caretaking mandate. If "the earth is the Lord's" (Psalm 24:1), surely he doesn't consider it a good return on investment to be presented

I've seen environmentalists hold the Bible aloft to blame it for every polluted stream and destroyed landscape. Likewise, I've heard Christians ridicule environmentalists as anti-capitalist, un-American, earth-worshipping whackos. Just a week ago, I listened to a prominent preacher say he was an avid earth-firster: log the earth first, then log the other

---

*Joel Salatin and his family run Polyface Farm in Swoope, Virginia. His newest book, his twelfth, is* The Marvelous Pigness of Pigs: Respecting and Caring for All God's Creation *(HarperOne, 2016).*

a creation of eroded soil, unbreathable air, and polluted waterways.

The Bible is full of admonitions regarding earth stewardship. From Adam and Eve taking care of the garden, to God's command to the Israelites not to chop down fruit trees when they entered the Promised Land, to Jesus' words about his Father numbering the sparrows, godly living grows out of visceral relationships between people and the planet.

I believe part of the Christian mandate is to use our intellectual capacity and mechanical ability to be God's hands and feet in redeeming the earth, remedying the devastation wrought by humankind. The principles and patterns established by God, clearly demonstrated through ecology, are not opposed to biblical principle; in fact, they corroborate it. The way that farmers large and small choose to farm impacts the way we eat. What's on our plate is not just inert stuff. Shouldn't food, and, by extension, farming, actually be a manifestation of God's provision and grace in our lives?

As a farmer, I ask myself: When people visit my farm, do they see a physical representation of biblical truth? That is, do they see forgiveness, mercy, abundance, glory, and neighborliness? Or do they see an outfit that runs roughshod over its neighbors, creating stench and pollution thoughtlessly excused as "smelling like money"? If being a good neighbor means anything, it should include not stinking up the community with huge volumes of fecal waste from confined animal feeding operations. And what about pesticides and

chemical fertilizers? It's hard to see how we're honoring the sanctity of life if most of what we apply to our food ends in the suffix *–cide,* meaning *killing.*

To help understand what's at stake, let's take a look at the word *glory.* Christians tend to assume that certain words in the Bible are spirit-speak, and *glory* is one such word. After all, who talks about glory in everyday conversation? Usually we restrict it to spiritual contexts such as the angels' announcement of Christ's birth: "Glory to God in the highest." Glory, we think, belongs to the invisible spirit world, and we speak of it only in hushed cathedral tones; by contrast, we view physical, visible things as lacking a moral dimension.

But the Bible does not make this modern distinction between the spiritual and the physical. In fact, in Scripture the word *glory* describes terrestrial things more often than celestial ones – it speaks, for instance, of the glory of nations, kings, old people, and young men and women. In biblical usage, *glory* means the true essence of something: its distinctiveness and uniqueness. Accordingly, when we bring glory to God, we recognize and accentuate the virtues that make him divine: we recognize that nothing else in the universe is immutable, sovereign, without beginning, omniscient, omnipresent, holy, and perfect.

These are lofty thoughts. But I propose that the best way to appreciate God's specialness is to first appreciate the physical specialness of his creatures. To give a flesh-and-blood

When people visit my farm, do they see biblical truth? That is, do they see forgiveness, mercy, abundance, glory, and neighborliness?

# Polyface Logic

Joel Salatin's Polyface Farm includes one thousand acres of pasture as well as woodland in Swoope, Virginia.

**2 Pastured Beef.** Just as wild herds graze an area intensively and then move to greener pastures, Polyface's eight hundred head of beef cattle are moved onto a new grass paddock every day, using movable electric fencing. This model heals the land, thickens the forage, reduces weeds, stimulates earthworms, reduces pathogens, and increases nutritional qualities in the meat.

**1 The Salad Bar.** The foundation for everything at Polyface Farm is the "salad bar": the pasture's biodiverse mix of grasses and perennial broadleaves. A rich mix of species utilizes more of the soil's nutrients than a monoculture can, allowing herbivores to always fill their stomachs with quality food. It also boosts productivity and soil health.

**3 Topsoil Care.** In the United States, topsoil has been badly depleted by two centuries of tillage. The soil is a vibrant ecosystem of bacteria, fungi, and invertebrates that needs nurture. Cow dung recycles nutrients back into the ground, adding organic matter and boosting microbial life. Similarly, all other fertility sources from the farm, even entrails from slaughtering, are recycled back into the topsoil.

**4 Hens and Turkeys.** Following the cows come the laying hens and turkeys, which eat the larvae in the cow dung. Housed in an "Eggmobile" (portable henhouse), the hens are free to range across the pasture, eating bugs and parasites and sanitizing the pasture while providing thousands of eggs. The turkeys, based out of their "Gobbledygo" portable hoop house, grow fat for Thanksgiving.

**5 Pigaerator Pork.** The pigs at Polyface Farm have two vital tasks: building compost and creating new pastures. They burrow through the cows' winter bedding – a tasty mix of hay, woodchips, dung, and fermented grain kernels – aerating it and turning it into compost. During summer the pigs, kept in herds of around forty, help create new pastureland by rotationally grazing recently cleared forest.

**6 People-Centric Farming.** At Polyface, four generations live and work together. "People-centric" means avoiding chemical poisons and dangerous machinery so the farm is safe for kids, and also ensuring meaningful work for everyone. Since there are no noxious odors or pollution, visitors, students and interns can be welcomed. All produce is sold locally in order to build strong community ties.

For more information, visit the farm's website at *www.polyfacefarms.com*.

The author with his "pigaerator" herd

example: by learning to appreciate the pigness of the pig we will understand how to appreciate the Godness of God. To say this isn't sacrilege. Instead, it means humbly recognizing that how well we honor the least of these is linked to how well we are able to honor the greatest of these. It's the moral framework that teaches us to honor and respect the Tomness of Tom or the Maryness of Mary.

Today's industrial food system treats pigs as mechanical objects – as mere inanimate protoplasmic structures to be manipulated in whatever clever ways human hubris can think up. Once we find the pig's stress gene, for example, we extract it from the pig's chromosomes to enable us to demean the pig's habitat even more – after all, now the pig won't care. Can you imagine having that kind of thought toward another living creature – for example, a cat or a dog?

A pig is a living being created by God. Life, as we know, responds to life. Plants respond to human touch – and to music! – and this is even truer of animals. When I step into my pig pasture, the pigs naturally come toward me, warily at first, and then more boldly if I stay quiet and sit down on the ground. Within a minute they're snoodling on my shoes, chewing on my belt, and looking for a belly rub.

I've never washed my car and had it snoodle on my shoes. The steering wheel sure doesn't ask for a belly rub. That's the point: mechanical things have no personality, no communication. To think that we can treat living beings like so many machines, to grow them faster, fatter, bigger, cheaper without moral thought or consequence, is to demean this magnificent creation God made as an object lesson of spiritual truth.

Christians preach about the importance of finding and using our God-given talents and gifts. What are the talents of a pig? Unlike any other animal, the pig has a plow on its nose. Denying the pig a habitat that allows it to dig, to gambol in sunshine, and to have enough space and stimulation around to express its innate curiosity violates the very essence of its being – its glory. What kind of Christian witness is it to choose food that inherently demonstrates an anti-glory way of thinking and acting?

Imagine parents telling their children that the reason they were eating humanely raised pork instead of industrial meat was because they wanted to honor the pigness of the pig. These are the ways we can put ourselves in a frame of mind in which we give God all his due. If we can't even respect the parts of creation we see, how will we be able to respect what we don't see?

The sun shines on the earth to grow plants that inhale carbon dioxide and exhale oxygen, splitting off the carbon to form their vegetative bodies. Much of it gets sequestered in the soil. Chemical fertilizer destroys the wondrous community of microbial beings and larger critters (like earthworms) that inhabit the soil, trading in an amazing underground café of nutrients. To assault this community of beings with simplistic chemicals and harmful tillage is to spoil God's stuff. And all of it is God's stuff.

Are we leaving the soil richer, the water purer, and the air cleaner, as a result of our food and farming system? Are we respecting and honoring the distinctiveness, gifts, and talents of the plants and animals in this divine choreography? Or is our attitude one that says food and farming are just mechanistic parts of amoral enterprises?

Most pastors and church leaders will not touch this issue because to do so would mean dropping their hostility to environmentalism, and in many cases it would jeopardize their own political reality. What does a pastor do when, after a sermon on sustainability, his lead elder, who happens to grow Monsanto genetically modified corn and soybeans or who has a Tyson factory farm, becomes miserly at putting money in the offering plate? What about Christians who work for outfits dedicated to nutrient deficiency, junk food, and a mechanistic view toward DNA and life?

> By learning to appreciate the pigness of the pig we will understand how to appreciate the Godness of God.

This is a real tension, but it is the tension of truth breaking into spiritual consciousness. Repentance is not a one-shot deal; it's ongoing spiritual disturbance, which creates fertile soil to germinate new seeds of understanding. The parallels between creation care and spiritual faithfulness are both profound and myriad.

The sooner the Christian community dares to converse about how belief permeates food and farming, the sooner its credibility in the culture will increase. Without that conversation, and without that conversion, the creation worshippers will retain the high road, and the creator worshippers will retain their image as conquistadors.

*Dear God, help me to honor and steward your stuff not because I worship it, but because in doing so I express worship toward the One who owns it all.*

# Questions for Joel Salatin

The average American farmer is age fifty-seven. Why aren't more young people taking up farming?

**Joel Salatin:** Our culture sees being a farmer like being a janitor. The Jeffersonian intellectual agrarian has been replaced by the redneck hillbilly persona.

We get calls from parents of interns: "I sent my kid to college so he would get a decent job, not go out and put his hands in the dirt." There is this condescending spirit.

What they don't realize is that humility and common sense come with participating in the awesomeness of nature. That's why I'm a big fan of children's gardens. For a child, it's powerful to plant a tomato seed, nurture the plant, watch the bees pollinate the blossoms, and see the little green orb grow and turn red. And in the end, I get to eat it, and the juice runs down my elbow. I become aware of having a place in something much bigger than me. That's so much more profound than being the top points getter in Angry Birds.

When we move into a virtual thought pattern we lose our moorings. We forget that we are fundamentally dependent on literally trillions of mycorrhizae, mycelium, nematodes, and bacteria in the soil.

Your grandchildren are growing up on the same farm on which you raised your own two children, as part of a multi-generational enterprise. What advice do you have to parents about how to teach children to love to work?

First of all you have to like to work yourself. We have to appreciate that all we do, from cleaning the toilet to planting the tomato plant, is all sacred stuff. It is an extension of God's participatory hand in life. We do it all as unto the Lord.

Do the kids help on butchering day?

We have never sheltered our kids from the most visceral aspects of farming. We have pictures of our kids in diapers dragging chickens on butchering day. There is no aversion to it. We are born with a primal sense of life and death – it's just a fact that something has to die for something to live. In a compost pile microbes are ingesting and being ingested by others.

All of creation is pulsing with sentience: when the sunflower tracks the sun across the sky, when the maple tree withholds its sap in a windstorm so that if a big branch falls it will have enough sap to run to the wound. Appreciating these things elevates our reverence, awe, and wonder.

That's a paradoxical way to learn the value of life!

When you kill something on a video game, you wait five seconds and it gives you a new icon. But when you go out to the garden and the tomato plant is dead, that's it. When you slaughter a chicken, it won't wake up when you press a button. The gravity of that situation helps to create a frame of reference for how we interact with each other.

Sometimes we become so disconnected that we don't have a frame of context for what true sacrifice is. Part of blessing our food is being grateful for the sacrifice, whether it is a carrot, a pig, or a chicken. The ultimate purpose of living things is to give themselves for something else.

The ultimate gift we give to each other is that we sacrifice ourselves in service for each other. And then, of course, there can be no eternal life without the sacrifice of Christ. There's the ultimate example of life. ➤

---

Interview by Kevin Keiderling on June 29, 2016.
▶ Watch the interview or read it in full at *plough.com/salatin*.

# Editors' Picks

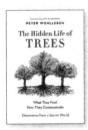

*The Hidden Life of Trees*
Peter Wohlleben
(Greystone)

**It turns out,** biologically speaking, that humans aren't all that exceptional. We finally decoded the genome, only to discover that we share 97 percent of it with the field mouse and 60 percent with the common fruit fly. A recent spate of pop-science books sets out to remind us not only that we are descended from fish and apes but, yes, that animals are people too. We now know that few of the things we thought made us special – language, technical ability, social and emotional complexity, a sense of time – are unique to our species. Carl Safina's *Beyond Words: What Animals Think and Feel* brings us dolphins and elephants that grieve. In *Are We Smart Enough to Know How Smart Animals Are?*, zoologist Frans de Waal implies that most zoologists preceding him were not, devising tests for clever bonobos and gibbons unjustly biased toward a human skill set. And Jennifer Ackerman's *The Genius of Birds* shows how much we have underestimated the bird brain. To anyone who's ever had a pet dog, none of these discoveries come as a great surprise.

Now this. Trees, too, may have feelings, and seemingly complex social lives as well. They love, grieve, talk, warn each other of danger, share resources with struggling neighbors, nurture their offspring, and support aging parents. When German forester Peter Wohlleben stopped going by the logging textbook and started listening to what his trees were trying to tell him, a whole new world opened up.

For one, the beeches native to his Central European forest actually want to grow closely together. If one tree is diseased or struggling on poor soil, its neighbors pass it nutrients, banding together to maintain the canopy that keeps sun and wind out and precious moisture in.

Each species competes ruthlessly with other species, and each has its natural enemies. Yet trees also enjoy a host of mutually beneficial relationships with fungi and insects. If attacked by a particular caterpillar, the oak releases a scent to summon a specific wasp to lays its eggs in the pests. Oaks and beeches throughout a forest can conspire to withhold their seeds for several years at a time to starve deer and boar populations that would otherwise eat all the acorns and beechnuts. When giraffes come to browse, umbrella thorn acacias start producing a foul-tasting toxin in their leaves. They also release a gas, ethylene, onto the breeze to alert nearby trees to start producing the same toxin. (The giraffes have learned to skip a few trees or move upwind.)

When it comes to how trees "think" or where their "brain" or "memory" resides, Wohlleben veers into speculation. He notes that not unlike our own neurons, roots have been overheard transmitting electrical impulses – at 220 hertz – to which other plants react, and that scientists now believe these communications are facilitated by a "wood-wide web" of fungal mycelium. Whether or not such comparisons to human intelligence are overblown, Wohlleben's fascinating book is a good place to start to recover a sense of wonder toward the created world around us.

*Unashamed*
LeCrae
(B&H)

**Where are unchurched millennials** hearing a gospel-informed perspective on society, politics, and culture? Many are likely getting it from Lecrae, the hip hop artist who is proving that violence, profanity, misogyny, and bling are not the only values that can top charts and win Grammys. (Watch his "Welcome to America" for starts.)

For more than a few chapters of his life – and of his recent memoir, *Unashamed* – Lecrae Devaughn Moore was a mess. Of course this makes his Christian testimony all the more compelling. Here's someone who, through the saving grace of Jesus Christ, overcame fatherlessness and sexual abuse, the pull of gangs, addiction and rehab, promiscuity and an abortion, racism and self-hatred, an unsteady relationship with religion, and some basic misconceptions about what it means to be a Christian. He became a Christian celebrity, making Christian music for Christian audiences, until he felt a call to break out of the Christian ghetto.

"There is no such thing as Christian rap and secular rap," LeCrae says now. "Only people can become Christians." He's had some degree of success in crossing the divide, though he senses that he'll always be an outsider in both worlds. The title track of his 2014 hit album, *Anomaly,* ends, "And they say we don't fit in / But I say, we are exactly who God created us to be: anomalies / The system didn't plan for this." Not a bad place for a Christian to be.

*Where the River Bends: Considering Forgiveness in the Lives of Prisoners*
Michael T. McRay
(Cascade)

**Not every story of childhood** trauma ends happily. The overall effect of these fourteen profiles of prisoners is devastating.

McRay studied peacemaking with visions of addressing the Israeli–Palestinian conflict, but felt as an American he had to do something to put his own house in order first. This led to a four-year stint as a volunteer chaplain at Riverbend Maximum Security Institution in Nashville, the sort of place we as a society have sought to put a festering wound "out of sight and out of mind."

The first part of the book maps out the complex topography of forgiveness. It comes off a little dry but provides a helpful framework for the rich stories that follow, which McRay lets the prisoners tell for themselves. Seven men and seven women, they take responsibility for their actions and express remorse, but as perpetrators cannot demand forgiveness of their victims. They are left struggling to forgive themselves. Some can't, such as the mother whose child died of neglect while she had postpartum psychosis; she refuses to appeal her sentence because she feels she deserves to stay in prison.

No story starts or ends the day of the crime. Almost inevitably, the victimizer was first a victim; the abuser was abused. Often their own inability to forgive horrific childhood or domestic abuse led them to perpetuate the cycle.

These are hard stories to hear, because they reveal as much about us as about the people we lock away. Jacob Davis, thirty-six, has served seventeen years of a life sentence for shooting a high school classmate. He asks, "Are we still human? Is there any forgiveness, any redemption for those who have truly repented? If not, what does that say about us all?" ➤ *The Editors*

*Read Michael McRay's account of a day on a maximum security mental health pod at plough.com/mcray.*

## Insight

### GEORGE MACDONALD

Man finds it hard to get what he wants, because he does not want the best; God finds it hard to give, because he would give the best, and man will not take it.

From George MacDonald, "Life," *Unspoken Sermons, Series 2* (Longmans, Green, 1886).

# An Apology for Vivian

I am afraid, Vivian,
that my words
will find themselves alone,
shivering cold on a park bench
as evening slows,
solemnly draped over the brownstones
and the parking meters
and over you, Vivian.

I am afraid that poetry
pays only the airy show:
condensed breath firstly warm,
thinning finely into evening's hollow cold.
Going unnoticed to the passers-by,
does it go so to you, Vivian?

I have seen your little body
fraying in the wind of its cancer.
I had hoped,
I had tasked my words to mend you, but,

Vivian, I am afraid
that poetry arrives impotent,
or, it seems, not at all —
having lost itself in a metaphor,
on a park bench,
cold, somnolent
and unemployed.

*JOSEPH MICHAEL FINO*

**ROGER MIELKE**

# Stewarding Mercy

## *The Role of Churches in the Refugee Crisis*

*As a senior official of the Evangelical Church of Germany, the country's national Protestant church, Dr. Roger Mielke is a leading spokesman for a Christian approach to public policy. We asked him how German churches are responding to the massive changes sweeping their country.*

How should Christian churches respond to the unique and urgent challenge of the refugee crisis? What is the special responsibility of the body of Christ – including the major churches, religious orders and communities, and individual Christians – one year after the opening of Germany's borders, which resulted in the influx of more than a million refugees and migrants? And what does the New Testament have to say about what the church's political witness should be and how it can be lived out?

### *Where We're At Today*

Before tackling these questions, it would be good to review the events of the past year from a political perspective, and explain the role churches have played so far.

Though the refugee crisis in Europe may seem to have burst out of the blue, already in

2012, when the civil war in Syria escalated, relief organizations and political experts were warning of a looming humanitarian disaster including mass displacement of populations. There had been similar warnings about Libya since 2011, when its government disintegrated into factional violence following the Western military intervention. Because of Libya's continued instability, it became the launching ground for refugees making their way to Europe across the Mediterranean. Human traffickers organized crossings in overloaded and haphazardly constructed vessels; each year thousands of refugees lost their lives making this journey.

Italy was left with the burden of receiving the refugees who survived the crossing, with precious little help offered from other European Union nations. No country was more emphatic than Germany in rejecting Italy's pleas for a quota system that would distribute refugees among EU member states. Instead, Italy's neighbors insisted on enforcing the so-called "Dublin system," whereby the first EU country that receives a refugee must accept responsibility for his or her future.

At the end of summer 2015, the refugee situation was worsening dramatically. Drastic cuts were made to monthly food rations in the refugee camps in the Middle East supported by the United Nations. This threw camp residents into total hopelessness, compounded by a lack of access to education or jobs. Now in addition to the main Mediterranean route, refugees also started traveling into Central Europe by way of the Balkans. Their way led through Greece, Macedonia, Serbia, Croatia, and Hungary as they sought to reach Germany, Sweden, Austria, and (to a lesser extent) the Netherlands.

By early autumn, the Dublin system had largely collapsed. Italy began allowing refugees arriving on the small island of Lampedusa to continue northward without registration. Likewise, Greece, Croatia, Hungary, and Austria started sidestepping refugee registration, contravening the Dublin rules. The horrifying image of the drowned two-year-old refugee boy Alan Kurdi, whose boat capsized while crossing from the Turkish mainland to the Greek island of Lesbos, shocked the world and became a symbol of the need for humanitarian action.

It was about the same time, in September 2015, that ten thousand refugees from Syria became stranded in Hungary. The Hungarian police rounded them up and held them at a train station in Budapest. In the midst of what had become an extremely explosive situation, German chancellor Angela Merkel agreed to allow these ten thousand refugees into her country. The floodgates had opened.

Initially, Merkel probably intended her decision as a one-time humanitarian gesture aimed at encouraging a generous policy by other European nations. News photographs of trains arriving in Munich filled with the refugees from Budapest went global. The chancellor welcomed the refugees and encouraged her fellow Germans to stand ready to help them: "Germany is a strong country. We can manage this."

Many Germans embraced this *Willkommenskultur* (culture of welcome). Throughout the country, ordinary people

> *"Germany is a strong country. We can manage this."*
>
> Angela Merkel, September 2015

---

*Dr. Roger Mielke is a member of the High Consistory of the Evangelical Church of Germany (EKD), where he leads the Office for Questions of Public Responsibility.*

opened their hearts and their homes. Volunteers and authorities worked together with surprising efficiency and effectiveness, despite the inevitable problems that arose as ten thousand people crossed into Germany each day between October 2015 and early February 2016.

*Germany has taken in 1.3 million refugees – an event that will permanently transform the country.*

In real terms, the border was now open; border controls were extremely minimal. What had been intended as a one-time humanitarian gesture became a lasting state of affairs. Public discussion pivoted from *Willkommenskultur* to the less rosy term *Kontrollverlust* (loss of control).

The influx only slowed when, as a result of prompting from Austria, first Macedonia and then the other Balkan states closed their borders to refugees. (Hungary had already cordoned off its borders to Croatia in mid-winter, a move that earned a sharp rebuke from the German government.) April 2016 saw the implementation of the European Union's deeply problematic and much-criticized agreement with Turkey to reduce the number of refugees fleeing via Greece and the Balkan route. By that time, in the period between September 2015 and March 2016, about 1.3 million people had entered Germany. The exact number is still unknown because many failed to register with the authorities (some perhaps deliberately), while others continued their journey toward Scandinavia, the Netherlands, and the United Kingdom.

By the summer of 2016, the once-overwhelming support for Merkel's policy of *Willkommenskultur* was giving way to deep divisions. Polls in July showed that 83 percent of Germans regard the influx of refugees as the nation's biggest political problem. The refugee crisis has become a key issue in regional elections for those who favor the right-wing populist party Alternative for Germany (AFD).

The symptoms of the breakdown of *Willkommenskultur* have a kind of symmetry. On one hand we see an alarming number of attacks on refugees and their housing, and on the other hand there have been the New Year's Eve assaults on women in Cologne by immigrant young men and terrorist attacks committed by migrants. Worries that the German state was losing control were only underlined when, after July's coup attempt in Turkey, voters watched as mass demonstrations of immigrants battled out domestic Turkish political disputes on the streets of German cities.

The polarization of German society comes at a time when the institutions of the European Union, which could play a fruitful role in the refugee situation, have become increasingly paralyzed. The EU debt crisis, an outgrowth of basic flaws in the European monetary union, is far from over; the European Central Bank's current policy of quantitative easing is only postponing the day of reckoning. Meanwhile, youth unemployment in Southern Europe is stagnating at a level that jeopardizes the legitimacy of the entire political system. Europe is also split over how to address the war in eastern Ukraine and how to confront Russia. And increasing centrifugal forces within the EU are threatening to divide it further, as Brexit demonstrates; several other European governments are anxious about upcoming elections in 2017.

Germany's place within the EU is marked by increasing isolation as a result of Merkel's response to the refugees. Her policies have met with rejection, ranging from cool rebuffs from the French and British to the enraged,

Photograph by Jörg Carstensen / EPA

resentment-laden protests of Eastern European nations. These countries argue that they cannot be expected to share in bearing the consequences of a crisis that they regard as caused by Merkel's recklessness, pointing out that Germany neither consulted them in advance nor involved them in decision making.

Many of the 1.3 million refugees will likely seek to remain in Germany, a demographic shift that will transform the country. What's more, asylum law permits family members to join an eligible asylum seeker in Germany. It's not surprising that some German citizens react to the prospect of the coming social shift with withdrawal, fear, aggression, or an exclusionary stance. From their perspective, the already painful pressures that the globalized economy has brought to bear are now being aggravated by the mass influx of refugees.

Between this position and that of the *Willkommenskultur* runs a fault line along which German and European politics will play out for the foreseeable future. Political elites will do well to offer policies that are plausible to a broad base of their electorates rather than reacting with their own forms of exclusion toward those unwilling or unable to follow the liberal mainstream.

## German Churches in Action

From the beginning of the refugee influx, German churches have seen themselves as an integral part of the *Willkommenskultur*. Bishop Heinrich Bedford-Strohm, chairman of the Evangelical Church in Germany (EKD), and Cardinal Marx of Munich, chairman of the German Catholic Bishops' Conference, both joined Merkel at Munich's main station to welcome the first trainloads of refugees.

Across the country, German churches and parishes have formed the backbone of civil society's efforts to care for the refugees sent to cities and villages after their initial processing. In many German towns, "round tables" have served as forums for local citizens to discuss and solve questions of how to receive and

Pro-refugee demonstrators protest a right-wing populist march in Berlin (July 2016).

The leaders of Germany's Catholic and Protestant churches welcome the first trainloads of refugees in Munich (September 2015).

Photograph: Johannes Minkus / FPD

integrate refugees, supply their immediate needs, and deal with any problems that arise. Local churches generally play a significant role in these forums, possessing as they often do a strong anchoring in community and regional affairs.

The major churches' public statements since summer 2015 have been insistent in urging Germans to embrace a culture of mercy, humanity, acceptance, open-mindedness, and diversity. In fact, by autumn 2015 the churches' official appeals had come to emphasize a language of human rights similar to that of the No Border movement, which demands freedom of movement as a fundamental human right and ultimately regards national states and borders as unjustified encroachments on this freedom. If anything, the Catholic Church has encouraged openness to migrants even more strongly than the (socially more liberal) Protestant churches. Perhaps Catholic theology's essentially critical view of nationhood plays a role here, as does its emphasis on the natural-law basis for human rights. Pope Francis's emphatic advocacy has only cemented this tendency.

What unites both Catholic and Protestant churches, however, is a resolute rejection of the right-wing populists and their penchant for invoking Christianity as a touchstone of German cultural identity. For instance, church leaders have denounced the populist slogan calling on Germans to defend the "Christian Occident." This consensus has been shared by evangelicals, a group that, despite enjoying a certain influence thanks to numbers and commitment levels, is often marginalized in a landscape dominated by the national Protestant church. While evangelicals have highlighted issues such as the persecution of Christians by Muslims or attacks on Christians housed in refugee homes, they have also taken on board the need for structural changes to German churches and congregations in order to reflect a more diverse society.

In the public square, what has lent special

credence to the voice of German churches is their direct links to churches in Iraq and Syria. This gives churches a unique form of firsthand access to reports about refugees' experiences of war, terrorism, and displacement. Yet it must be said, too, that the churches' appeals for a sustainable foreign policy to address the root causes of the crisis have been largely ineffectual, partly because their recommendations to the government have fluctuated, at times calling for a nonviolent solution and at times giving a tentative blessing to the use of military force.

Nor will the churches long be able to ignore the public's growing skepticism toward immigration and the social changes it portends. After all, this skepticism is already surfacing among their members.

## Mercy and Stewardship

The obligation to care for the vulnerable and marginalized lies at the heart of Scripture, especially its teaching about the Trinity: the community of love that exists within God himself as Father, Son, and Holy Spirit. God, by his very nature, is a relationship-seeking God whose life is one of communion. This love overflows itself. By calling Israel out from among the nations and accompanying her through history, God opens a way for a fallen and hostile humanity to share in his life of love. Through the cross of Jesus, the incarnate eternal Son of God, this suffering and vulnerable love overcomes evil, renews human beings through the Holy Spirit, and destines them for eternal life in communion with the Triune God within his transformed creation.

This very brief summary of the biblical gospel offers the most fundamental basis for shaping a response to the refugee crisis. Jesus Christ commands his community of disciples to go with him on his way of suffering love and reconciliation. He frees them from their compulsion to pursue their own self-serving interests in competition; he frees them to serve. Like him, they are to receive and care for the lost, the wounded, and those in need of protection. In every suffering human face, the body of Christ is to see Jesus himself. The church is to encounter each person with an unconditional commitment that extends far beyond the circle of fellow Christians, reaching out to include every person as a creation of God who, though lost, is someone Jesus came to save. As Matthew 25:40 teaches, "Whatever you did for one of the least of these brothers and sisters of mine, you did for me."

*In every suffering human face, the body of Christ is to see Jesus himself.*

This passage, which contains the core of the New Testament's attitude toward those most in need of care and protection, is set in a framework that is significant: that of the farewell discourses in Matthew 23–25. If we're attentive to this framework, it can teach us how we as the body of Christ should discern the signs of the times and understand our task in the political realm. Here at the end of Matthew's Gospel, Jesus, faced with death on the cross, confronts the political and religious elite of his day, proclaiming to them the imminent end of their power. He puts the political realm into the context of the end times, announcing: The kingdoms of this world will come to an end; they are destined to pass away. But the kingdom of the crucified and risen one has arrived.

According to Matthew, then, political affairs belong to the interim period that will conclude with Jesus' return at the end of time. This interim period is a time of confrontation between evil – which, though conquered, still remains powerful – and the kingdom of

God, which was inaugurated at Pentecost. In Matthew 23–25, Jesus teaches his disciples, and through them the body of Christ today, the ethic that should guide their political role during this interim. Though it's only possible here to sketch out the main contours of this ethic, its main features include:

- the insight that the body of Christ has been stationed in a disintegrating, and therefore violent, world. The church is to confront this violence with nonviolence and with the spirit of suffering love;

- the clear conviction that only a close relationship with Jesus and loyalty to him will enable us to stand firm in our confrontation with evil;

- the practice of mercy, that is, the foundational virtue of providing love and care to the hungry, thirsty, homeless, naked, sick, and imprisoned.

In accordance with this ethic, there is only one possible way for the body of Christ to respond to the vulnerable and marginalized, including today's refugees and migrants: with unconditional love. In a nutshell: we must practice mercy.

*The church must oppose both kinds of exclusion, whether from the left or the right.*

Yet that is not all that Matthew 23–25 can teach us about the Christian's role in politics. There is a second lesson, found in Matthew 25:1–30, that we must also take to heart. Here Jesus tells two parables that deal with boundaries and limited capabilities: the Parable of the Ten Virgins and the Parable of the Talents. Here Jesus calls for the prudent use of the natural and spiritual talents entrusted to us – precisely because we are accountable to him for how we use them. Wisdom in using these talents is expressed both through practicing generosity and through remaining aware of our own limits.

We could call this an ethic of stewardship.

Jesus' message in these two parables is in accord with the interim nature of politics: "The present form of this world is passing away" (1 Cor. 7:31). In this transitory world, God has instituted ordinances to restrain the power of evil, ordinances to which, for the time being, both believers and nonbelievers are subject. The relationship of the body of Christ to the state, then, must be one of distance – but also one of loyalty.

How does this look in practice? We can gain insight by examining the role of human rights. Though the origins of the concept of human rights are diverse, any attempted genealogy will end up acknowledging that the two most important sources are (1) the Enlightenment's rationalistic theory of natural law and (2) the core biblical axiom that every human being is created in the image of God, and so enjoys an inalienable dignity.

Human rights, by their very nature, precede the political realm and all positive law; they remain valid regardless of whether a given political regime recognizes them or not. Nonetheless, these rights remain empty without a political community that enforces them in a concrete way, enshrining them as both the source and the measure of its laws.

This is why the Christian church has such a strong interest in the healthy functioning of the political community surrounding it and of the rule of law. In most of the world today, the political community can only function healthily if it is secured by democratic legitimacy, usually expressed in the form of a national state. Since this is so, the church cannot regard the national state in which it finds itself as something foreign. Rather, the ethic of stewardship demands that the church see itself as both responsible for, and loyal to, the state. Exactly this is what the ethic of stewardship demands.

How can we apply these principles to the refugee crisis? A sizable number of German voters (and even bigger percentages elsewhere in Europe) believe that the forced acceptance of so many refugees and migrants is endangering the healthy functioning of their country. This viewpoint expresses itself through increased polarization, rising rates of violence, and voting results that have given populist parties political influence (even while leaving them outside national or regional governments). Such a polarized environment allows the logic of exclusion to start determining political reality. In an ugly symmetry, exclusion of immigrants on the one side mirrors the exclusion of right-wingers on the other.

To be sure, we must welcome our fellow citizens' renewed engagement in political affairs, coming as it does after a long period of executive and technocratic domination of political life. Yet there are dangers. Political passions can easily undermine social solidarity, lead to exclusionary politics, and threaten the healthy functioning of the political community.

The Christian church must vigorously oppose both kinds of exclusion, whether from the left or the right. Our task as the body of Christ is summed up well in the saying: "You are in the world but not of the world" (John 17). In other words, the church must act out of a deep commitment to care for the vulnerable by showing mercy – and yet at the same time, it must concern itself with the health of the political community to which it belongs with a commitment that is almost (!) equally deep.

The ethic of mercy and the ethic of stewardship are both in their own way anchored in the heart of the gospel. Both need to be reflected and balanced in the public witness and practical actions of the body of Christ. At the end of the day, however, the political realm will have passed away, bearing as it does the mark of the transitory. What will remain is mercy. ⟿

*Translated from German by Peter Mommsen and Dr. Andries Conradie.*

Rally of the populist movement PEGIDA (Patriotic Europeans against the Islamization of the Occident) in Dresden (February 2016).

# Learning to Love Goodness

## *In Praise of George MacDonald*

**MARIANNE WRIGHT**

IN A WIDELY REPRODUCED photo-graph from an 1876 book titled *English Celebrities of the Nineteenth Century,* George MacDonald appears among a group of nine British literary giants.[1] Charles Dickens is there, of course, as well as Anthony Trollope, Wilkie Collins, and W. M. Thackeray. The photograph – a montage created by a commercial publisher – is a visual monument to Victorian eminence: big black-cloaked men with big beards who wrote big, famous books.

When this picture was first published, it was apparently uncontroversial to rank George MacDonald among the great writers of his age. Not so today. It has been at least a century since MacDonald has been widely read, and scholars outside his small fan base tend to approach his works as period pieces rather than as literature. So it is reasonable to ask: can we truly consider MacDonald a great writer?

C. S. Lewis, like many of MacDonald's admirers, had his doubts, writing that: "MacDonald has no place in [literature's] first rank – perhaps not even in its

second."[2] Today's reader, when first confronted with MacDonald's writing, may well be tempted to agree. His books are long, his nineteenth-century mannerisms do not all age well, and several of his novels include patches of intimidating Scots dialect.

All this. Yet mention MacDonald's name, and it will not be long before you find yourself speaking with someone who, like C.S. Lewis, has found MacDonald's books "beyond price" despite their literary deficiencies.[3] Lewis goes on:

> I dare not say that he is never in error; but to speak plainly I know hardly any other writer who seems to be closer, or more continu-ally close, to the Spirit of Christ Himself. Hence his Christ-like union of tenderness and severity. Nowhere else outside the New Testament have I found terror and comfort so intertwined.[4]

I was introduced to George MacDonald early in life by my grandfather, Richard Arnold Mommsen. He could read aloud better than

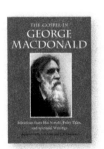

*This article is taken from the introduction to the new Plough title* The Gospel in George MacDonald: Selections from His Novels, Fairy Tales, and Spiritual Writings, *ed. Marianne Wright (2016). The author is a contributing editor to this magazine.* plough.com/macdonald

anyone in the world, and among the dozens of books he read to me and my siblings were MacDonald's *At the Back of the North Wind, The Princess and the Goblin,* and *The Princess and Curdie.* My grandparents' house was full of books, but it was obvious even to a child that George MacDonald meant something special to him. At a time when most of MacDonald's books were out of print and difficult to find, Grandpa would spend long weekend afternoons combing the catalogs of secondhand booksellers for titles he hadn't read. The books, when they came, were generally in poor condition. He mended and rebound them with loving precision, letting us help paint on the stiff bindery glue and select ribbons to bind in as markers. Into the back of each book he pasted a glossary of Scottish terms, and in the front he placed a photo-copied overview of MacDonald's life along with a list of his works. The list was annotated in Grandpa's decisive handwriting to save future readers from wasting time on titles he considered inferior. There are marks of A plus for his favorites (*Robert Falconer, Sir Gibbie, Warlock o' Glenwarlock*). *Lilith,* which he could never see the point of, rates a D minus.

Like many people who love MacDonald's writings, Grandpa made collections of extracts. It was from one of these – ninety-one short selections manually typed on a vintage Smith Corona and bound into a little volume he gave my father for his birthday – that I first discovered, at a time when I badly needed

> "A little more of God will make up for a good deal less of you."
>
> *George MacDonald*

it, MacDonald's great-hearted, practical, but uncompromising account of the New Testament message. I read that collection numerous times before I read MacDonald's novels for myself, and, although I have since read almost all his published work, I still return to that little book for inspiration and reflection.

✦ ✦ ✦

That George MacDonald is known at all today is likely due to the influence his writings had on two of the twentieth century's most important Christian apologists, G. K. Chesterton and C. S. Lewis. Both men gladly acknowledged their debt to him, and both were eager that he should be more widely read. Chesterton wrote, "When he comes to be more carefully studied as a mystic, as I think he will be when people discover the possibility of collecting jewels scattered in a rather irregular setting, it will be found, I fancy, that he stands for a rather important turning point in the history of Christendom."[5] For both men, MacDonald's imaginative stories first provided a new view of the world: Chesterton described *The Princess and the Goblin* as "a book that has made a difference to my whole existence,"[6] while C. S. Lewis said that after reading *Phantastes* as a young atheist, "I knew that I had crossed a great frontier."[7] Lewis went on to explain this when he looked back later in life:

> The quality which had enchanted me in his imaginative works turned out to be the quality of the real universe, the divine,

magical, terrifying, and ecstatic reality in which we all live. I should have been shocked in my teens if anyone had told me that what I learned to love in *Phantastes* was goodness. But now that I know, I see there was no deception. The deception is all the other way round – in that prosaic moralism which confines goodness to the region of Law and Duty, which never lets us feel in our face the sweet air blowing from "the land of righteousness."

As Lewis indicates, for MacDonald the ordinary events of each day – the "holy present," as he called it – are messages to us direct from God. He was convinced that the kingdom of heaven can be a reality in the here and now, and that it requires daily acts of obedient discipleship to bring it about. As a character in his novel *Thomas Wingfold* puts it: "I begin to suspect . . . that the common transactions of life are the most sacred channels for the spread of the heavenly leaven."[8]

This quote was one of several that my grandfather never tired of repeating. In May

> "If you do not obey Him, you will not know Him. . . . Obedience to Christ is Christianity. Let me die insisting upon it. For my Lord insists upon it."
>
> *George MacDonald*

2002 he was found to have advanced incurable cancer. During his final summer, his appreciation for the joys of daily life remained vivid, but he never (that I know) questioned or regretted that his time on earth was ending.

During those months he referred us to a passage from one of MacDonald's A-plus titles, *What's Mine's Mine*, that could have been written about him: "I do care to live – tremendously, but I don't mind where. He who made this room so well worth living in, may surely be trusted with the next!"

Love of life and an uncomplicated trust in its Author: these are the gifts George MacDonald offers his readers. In an age when the daily news seems increasingly complex and terrible, it is high time for many more to discover with him the joy and promise of simple discipleship. As he wrote to a friend near the end of his life: "Then hail to the world with all its summers and snow, all its delight and its aching, all its jubilance and its old age. We shall come out of it the sons and daughters of life, of God himself the only Father."

1. *English Celebrities of the Nineteenth Century* (London: Hughes and Edmonds, 1876).

2. C.S. Lewis, preface to *George MacDonald: An Anthology,* ed. C. S. Lewis (London: Geoffrey Bles, 1946).

3. C. S. Lewis to Edith Gates, May 23, 1944, in *The Collected Letters of C.S. Lewis*, vol. 2, ed. Walter Hooper (Harper Collins, 2004), 616.

4. C. S. Lewis, preface.

5. G. K. Chesterton, introduction to *George MacDonald and his Wife* (London: Allen & Unwin, 1924), 13.

6. Ibid.

7. C. S. Lewis, preface.

8. George MacDonald, *Thomas Wingfold, Curate* (London: Hurst and Blackett, 1876).

# Who Invented Thirst and Water?

## GEORGE MACDONALD

What, I ask, is the truth of water? Is it that it is formed of hydrogen and oxygen? . . . There is no water in oxygen, no water in hydrogen: it comes bubbling fresh from the imagination of the living God, rushing from under the great white throne of the glacier. The very thought of it makes one gasp with an elemental joy no metaphysician can analyze.

The water itself, that dances, and sings, and slakes the wonderful thirst – symbol and picture of that draught for which the woman of Samaria made her prayer to Jesus – this lovely thing itself, whose very wetness is a delight to every inch of the human body in its embrace – this live thing which, if I might, I would have running through my room, yea, babbling along my table – this water is its own self, its own truth, and is therein a truth of God.

Let him who would know the love of the maker, become sorely athirst and drink of the brook by the way – then lift up his heart – not at that moment to the maker of oxygen and hydrogen, but to the inventor and mediator of thirst and water, that man might foresee a little of what his soul may find in God. If he become not then as a hart panting for the water-brooks, let him go back to his science and its husks. . . . As well may a man think to describe the joy of drinking by giving thirst and water for its analysis, as imagine he has revealed anything about water by resolving it into its scientific elements.

Let a man go to the hillside and let the brook sing to him till he loves it, and he will find himself far nearer the fountain of truth than the triumphal car of the chemist will ever lead the shouting crew of his half-comprehending followers. He will draw from the brook the water of joyous tears, "and worship him that made heaven, and earth, and the sea, and the fountain of waters."

*Taken from* The Gospel in George MacDonald: Selections from His Novels, Fairy Tales, and Spiritual Writings, *ed. Marianne Wright (Plough, 2016).* plough.com/macdonald

# Muhammad Ali

## JASON LANDSEL

"We all have the same God, we just serve him differently. . . . It doesn't matter whether you're a Muslim, a Christian, or a Jew. When you believe in God, you should believe that all people are part of one family. If you love God, you can't only love some of his children."

*Muhammad Ali*

Born January 17, 1942, in Louisville, Kentucky, Muhammad Ali rejected his "slave name," Cassius Marcellus Clay Jr., and converted to Islam at age twenty-two. Throughout his life, Ali made controversial choices, including his decision to ally himself with the Nation of Islam, an organization whose ideology was as incendiary in the 1960s as it is today. As Ali himself would admit, "The Greatest" was no saint, but his faith played a guiding role in his life.

In 1967, at the peak of his physical abilities, Ali – the heavyweight champion of the world – committed what many perceived as career suicide. At the height of the Vietnam War, Ali claimed conscientious objector status, refusing to be inducted into the US Army. "My conscience won't let me go shoot my brother, or some darker people, or some poor hungry people in the mud for big, powerful America. And shoot them for what? They never called me nigger, they never lynched me, they didn't put no dogs on me, they didn't rob me of my nationality, rape and kill my mother and father. . . . How can I shoot them poor people? Just take me to jail."

His dissent earned the rage of government officials and the sports community. The media branded him a traitor, and the courts convicted him of draft evasion, stripped him of his titles, and sentenced him to five years in prison. He was fined ten thousand dollars and was banned from boxing for three years.

But Ali's courage and his commitment to his faith did not go unrecognized. As William Rhoden, a *New York Times* columnist, wrote, "Ali's actions changed my standard of what constituted an athlete's greatness. Possessing a killer jump shot or the ability to stop on a dime was no longer enough. What were you doing for the liberation of your people? What were you doing to help your country live up to the covenant of its founding principles?"

Ali's spirituality continued to evolve and grow over the course of his lifetime, and he never shied away from confronting his own contradictions. Several years before his death, he wrote in his memoir, "Truly great people in history never wanted to be great for themselves. All they wanted was the chance to do good for others and be close to God. I'm not perfect. I know that I still have things to work out, and I'm working on them. There are certain things I have done that I am not proud of, especially when they caused pain to others. I ask God for forgiveness."

Speaking at the boxer's funeral earlier this year, comedian Billy Crystal defined Ali's legacy: "He was a tremendous bolt of lightning. . . . Muhammad Ali struck us in the middle of America's darkest night. His intense light shined on America and we were able to see clearly: injustice, inequality, poverty – and pride, self-realization, courage, laughter, love, joy, and religious freedom for all."

*Jason Landsel is the artist for* Plough's *"Forerunners" series, including the painting opposite.*